There's an Angel in my Computer

Straight Talk from Spirit
Book 1

Carol Gino

Copyright © 2010 Carol Gino
All rights reserved.

Published by aaha! Books
New York & Texas
www.starwater.com

ISBN-10: 1936530007
EAN-13: 9781936530007
LCCN: 2010903794

EPub ISBN: 9781936530014
Kindle ISBN: 9781936530021

Dedication

To all who listen for the whispers of the soul

Other books by Carol Gino
The Nurse's Story
Rusty's Story
Then An Angel Came

The Family by Mario Puzo-Completed
by Carol Gino

Prologue

The panoramic view of life doesn't only happen at the moment of death. It happens during every big change, every great grief, in any exquisitely beautiful moment. That's how it always was for me, anyway. Suddenly slices of my life play like a slide show on my inner projection screen, complete with sensation and emotion, and I can see my whole life unfolding with a chilling clarity.

The vision. I'm sure it began when I was a little kid and said my bedtime prayers without supervision or guidelines. Now that I'm grown up, I realize that little kids should never be allowed to pray alone. They're too sincere, too committed and they make lousy deals.

But I was a difficult child to stop once I set my heart on something. Even at seven, I was a mini-zealot. Each night, as I kneeled next to my bed, head down, hands pressed tightly together, eyes squeezed shut as I had seen in all the pictures of young saints, my voice filled with emotion as I pleaded, "Dear Lord, could I please have a vision and be a saint, like Bernadette?" Even then I was a big reader. I had memorized the stories of all small saints or children with visions. And

I was competitive. Each of them *knew* they were being *called*, each of their souls had been touched by God. So every night after I prayed, I waited and listened for the "call."

Night after night, I heard nothing. I would try to be patient but finally, disappointed, I'd take a deep breath and crawl into bed. I kept my eyes closed for what seemed like forever, fighting sleep, as I searched my "soul" to see if I was worthy–just as I'd been taught to by the nuns at Our Lady of Perpetual Help Catholic school.

I kept the faith and said my nightly prayers for years in the face of God's silence. By the time I was nine, I figured I needed a new strategy. I was ready to renegotiate. "Dear God, if I can't be a saint, then I'd like to at least be a nun. Forget the Prince, I'm okay with being married to God." I almost swooned with the mystery and romance of it all. Still, I heard nothing. I was a tenacious child, so I continued to bargain. "But if You are already married to too many nuns, then I'd like to be a lawyer."

Though time passed, I kept my resolve. Then one night when I couldn't stand the suspense any longer, I offered my version of surrender. "Whatever You choose for me, is fine with me. But if its true that I have free will like they say in the Bible, and I have a real choice about my life, I'd like to have a vision and I'd like to experience everything, if you don't mind."

My sister, Barbara, on the other hand, was a realist. She loved harmony and beauty, but had no use for visions. Four years younger than me, she understood from the beginning that I was asking for trouble. As I prayed for a vision, she kneeled right next to me and prayed, "God, when my sister gets her vision, could I *not* have one, please?"

Barbara was less dramatic and less driven than I was, but certainly just as fervent. Visions held none of the fascination for her that they did for me. I thought it was because she was younger, and she didn't get it yet. She was brought up on stories of the animal kingdom, Italian food and the beauty of nature, while I was fed philosophy, religious myth and fairy tales.

Each night at the dinner table I listened to my father, rapt, so enchanted that I could hardly chew, as he read another story or parable from the Bible, or a chapter of the Harvard classics on Heraclitus, Plato or some other great philosopher, while my sister rolled her peas around her plate bored to tears. The words of those Greek philosophers were so much more sacred than any words the parish priest spoke from the pulpit at Sunday Mass.

Well, it took some time but God answered my prayers and filled my life with everything. It didn't occur to me at seven that everything included both the good and the bad   Still, life is full of surprises. And the one surprise I want to share with you in this journal is how I finally got my vision and how creative the universe is in answering prayers.

First Contact

The day I met Rashana began like any other, I swear it did. I made regular tea rather than decaffeinated that morning, and I confess I sprinkled a little refined sugar on my oat bran cereal, but honestly, that's it. I did no drugs.

After I'd skimmed the newspaper–skimmed, because there's only so much bad news I can take before I start my day–I took my tea into the study and sat down at my computer. I was working on a magazine article, "Sex in Marriage: The New Way." I turned on some music, a soft rendition of Pachabel–I've found that music often stimulates my creativity. Before I started to type, though, I decided to check my email.

I had just started to read a few messages from friends, when an Instant Message interrupted me.

> *Dearest Cranberry,*
> *I would like permission to contact you regularly and transmit some information from Home. Do you accept?*
> *Love and Light,*
> *Rashana*

Cranberry? I thought, laughing to myself. Cute screen name, but it wasn't mine. I figured that someone had mixed up my email address with Cranberry's. So I typed the following message.

> To Whom It May Concern,
> I'm afraid there's been a mistake and that you've contacted someone other than "Cranberry." Better search for the correct email address and try again. Good Luck!

Before I knew it another message appeared on my screen.

> *Dearest Joyful Jaybird,*
> *I would prefer to be addressed by my proper name rather than "To Whom It May Concern." You know it concerns me or I would not have contacted you. In case you've forgotten, my name is Rashana. I have been working on this project for several time sequences and only need your permission to continue and connect. There has been no mistake.*
> *Love & Light,*
> *Rashana*

I tried to think. I was sure I didn't know anyone called Rashana. Even if we'd only met at a party or a conference, a name like that wouldn't just slip my mind. I was certain it was a mistake.

> Rashana,
> Forgive me, but I'm embarrassed to admit that I don't remember you. Could

you refresh my memory about where we met? And then could you explain what I can do for you?

My Dear Sight Unseen,
The reason I am trying to contact you is precisely because you don't remember me. I'd like to reintroduce myself so we can continue the journey we planned together before this life at hand. I want to offer something that I've been trying to give you for quite a while, but I have been unable to get your attention before now.
Love and Light,
Rashana

I searched my memory. No Rashana, I was certain. I went all the way back to the kids I knew in grade school, but Rashana wasn't something that people in the mostly white, middle-class Long Island town of Lindenhurst named their kids. I typed again....

Dear Rashana,
I am certain there is some mistake. But I'm often certain of things and still not right so I'd like to try to help correct it. Could you identify yourself a little more clearly? It's hard to recognize a person without any physical description and without being able to see him or her. And could you tell me your last name?

Dearest Sharp as a Tack,
Physical description? YOU are my face and my physical presence. That's the point.

Last name? The name RASHANA was given to me by the All-Knowledge when I began. It represents a vibration or a frequency. RASHANA is all that I am, except for you, of course.
Lighter Love,
Rashana

Rashana,
   Is this some sort of joke?

Dearest Precious Puzzle Piece,
   I asked the Thirteenth Master the same question. He/She assured me that this was all part of a Greater Plan. You included.

The Thirteenth Master? My imagination went wild. After all, the media was always warning us about all the terrible things that could befall those who surfed the net. I was getting nervous. All I needed was to find myself mixed up with some terrorist group. My family would never forgive me. I'd have to ask straight out.

Rashana,
   Do you belong to some secret organization? Are you from a foreign country? And if so, is it a democracy and a friend of the United States?

Dearest Patriotic Soul,
   What a wonder you are. Here I am sitting at the Computer of Manifestation transmitting from the University of Higher Thought

and you want to know where I'm from. I am a Creative Spirit and my specialty now is Creative Communication. As for our relationship? I am your Higher Self. An appropriate metaphor which may comfort you and not frighten you? From a belief system that is familiar? An Angel.
Your Spirit,
Rashana

I should have known. All that Love and Light stuff from someone I didn't even know. Probably some New Age nut, distracting me from my work. I was open to the idea of angels. It wouldn't even be my first encounter with an angel—if that's what Rashana really was. But as much as I liked my Mac computer, I didn't think they made software that could communicate with higher realms. Besides, Rashana wasn't acting like an angel. It was hard enough to write about Sex and Marriage without this. I'd have to put an end to it.

Rashana,
First of all, it's It's my understanding that angels are perfect. That means they are considerate, polite, compassionate and have higher wisdom. You'll forgive me if I say you sound kind of pushy to me.

Dearest Disenchanted Soul,
I've tried all those other aspects to no avail. Besides, "pushy" is a judgment call, and so is "perfect." Some angels are so perfect they don't make judgments, but if I were one

of those, you wouldn't be a soul on earth at this time. And as long as we're sharing our feelings, I must tell you that I have been trying for years to get your attention. The human race is in great difficulty now because too many souls are unaware of their higher connections. Each of us here on the spirit realm is trying, with great effort, I might add, to share with our souls on Earth the wisdom that will help them evolve and aid in the evolution of Mother Soul Earth.
Greater Love & Light,
Rashana.

The phone rang then and I jumped, but it was just somebody trying to sell me a new computer. Another computer? Who knows who'll be in that one? At least Rashana, whoever she was, had some interesting ideas, even if they were a bit delusional. I could live with that. I'd worked as a nurse in mental institutions and some of the biggest crazies I'd met had great truths to tell and interesting perspectives on life, so I decided to go with it and explore the possibilities. I typed again.

Rashana,
If I assume you're telling the truth, how did you get stuck in my computer?

Dearest Dense Matter,
Stuck? Stuck? I am assuming that you don't know that "stuck" is one of the greatest insults to a Spirit of Light. "Stuck" is stagnant, not moving, not flowing and not learning and growing, therefore it is the only

"evil," if you will, to those of a higher nature. I am not "stuck" in your computer any more than a TV newscaster is stuck in your TV. I am using the silicon chip to make contact, to create a bridge between my realm and yours, in the only way that you seem to be able to recognize. And on second thought, I must also take exception to you calling me pushy. It is only Masters of Illusion or earthbound souls who invade a person's space without their knowledge or permission.

I have identified myself as being from the Light, from the Thirteenth Master–or "God," as you on Earth like to call the Highest Lit One. I have tried for decades to encourage you to meditate, pray, and go inside your heart to find this wisdom. I have been patient but unsuccessful in all these attempts and so I have been forced to be creative in my communications. If I was "pushy" and "stuck" as you say, I would have just entered your consciousness, but that is not my nature. In fact, you are straining our relationship by making a spirit of my nature haunt you.
Even Greater Love,
Rashana

Okay, so now I had insulted someone I didn't even know and I felt bad about it. It could be somebody living alone somewhere, completely isolated, who had just gone a little crazy. After all my years of nursing, I still felt compassion for anyone who was in trouble, and this person seemed to need my help. I was afraid to sign off for fear "Rashana" would do something foolish or harmful to him or herself.

Rashana,
    This is an awkward question for me to ask, but it would help me get a clearer picture of you if you wouldn't mind answering it. Do you have a web page, with a picture? Are you on Facebook? And are you male or female?

Dearest Either/Or,
    I am both. Spirits of the Light are what human livings call androgynous. They have masculine aspects and feminine aspects, as well as many other aspects too numerous to mention. As a spirit who is always learning and growing and trying to integrate many of these aspects, I am pleased that you asked.
L&L
Rashana

Rashana,
    I know this must be tedious for you, but I'm still not sure how we're connected or where you're from. Can you explain more simply?

Dearest Pathfinder,
    In the beginning, or as far back as I seem to remember, there was the All-Knowledge or the Light. A spirit like myself, or the higher self, is a fragment of Light. When the lessons a spirit needs to learn can best be learned on

*Earth, that spirit takes on a soul. The spirit packs into that soul all the gifts it will need to accomplish its purpose and learn those lessons. Then while that spirit stays attached to the Light, its soul (in our case, you) incarnates out of the One or All Knowledge into denser matter (in our case, on Earth). And there the journey of Life and growth begins.
Lovingly,
Rashana*

Dear Rashana,
Are you saying that you really are my higher self? My spirit?

*My Dear Soul,
The missing piece, your longing. The reason for your homesickness and discontent is your ignorance of my presence in your life, always. And this piece is often misunderstood. I am your Higher Self, in Universal Reality. Angels are truly from another realm, a realm in which there isn't incarnation.
Love,
Rashana.*

I was more comfortable thinking of Rashana as an angel than as my higher self. I couldn't imagine what I would be like as my higher self. As my own lowly self, I had enough characteristics that made me nervous. But I had believed in angels since I was a child. Nonetheless, I had never heard of a spirit or an angel coming through a computer and so I was still wary. I figured I'd be able to tell if this was someone with an angelic nature by asking some pertinent questions.

> Rashana,
> Who makes the decisions about my life, you or me? Is my whole life predestined?

Dear Free Soul,
According to the Larger Story being written by the Great Spirit of Light—who, by the way, is perfect and therefore also contains imperfection—some plans are already decided and some you can input. The lessons we must learn together must be learned, yet some of the ways in which we must learn them are given as a choice to you as soul. But if you like, to relieve any worry on your part, I may say that in this life, at this time, the tune that you're singing is the song of the Healer and the dance you are doing is one of Joy.

> Rashana,
> One more question? What happens when I shut off my computer?

Dearest Pain in the Ask,
As always, the screen will darken and we will both move forward to other thoughts and activities.

◈

The following day, when I sat down to work I quickly got caught up in my writing, and it was hours before

I realized that I hadn't heard from Rashana again. To be honest, I was a little disappointed. I like "interesting" and once I got over my initial shock, I loved exploring new ideas. Besides, no one really had ever explained to my satisfaction where "creativity" came from, and I had a sneaking suspicion that's what was happening, so I was looking forward to exploring it further. But days went by without word from Rashana, and then weeks.

Winter was passing and the weather was beginning to change. Spring was beautiful that year, and in an attempt to develop increased awareness of nature, I decided to plant a vegetable garden in my backyard and add some flowers to the front of my house to brighten the landscape. I often find myself obsessed by the things I do, and all Spring I was completely absorbed by my planting, so the time seemed to fly by. In the back of my mind, I did think about Rashana a few times, but I was almost certain that what had happened wouldn't happen again. I thought of it as a creative accident.

Around the beginning of summer, I was starting a new book about women's friendships and my Thursday night meetings with several buddies I'd worked with in different hospitals–the nurses that I'd made composites of in my first book, *The Nurse's Story*.

When I write, my life takes on a different level of obsession. I get up early, stay up late and my characters play in my head. So one morning, early, I began to type, the words and thoughts flowing freely for the first time in a while. Suddenly the

IM icon in my dock began to jump up and down. I took a deep breath.

> *Dearest Brave Soul,*
> What a pleasure it was to finally be able to communicate with you. I was so joyful that I spent the space between our contacts decorating the skies with new and shiny stars. You cannot imagine what a sense of happiness a spirit has when we are finally able to make our souls on earth aware of our presence in their lives. I spent that space just imagining what we could do together if you are willing. How we could, in our own small way, quicken evolution and beautify the landscape of consciousness on earth in the same way that you have done with your flowers. I was with you while you planted, and you will see the difference in the way your flowers grow. Then you will have some idea of the beautiful things we can accomplish while you are living on Earth.
> *Love & Light,*
> *Rashana*

I could feel myself frowning. I'm not sure if I was more annoyed or more frightened. On some level I'm sure I still didn't even believe she was a spirit. At any rate, if this relationship was going to continue, some ground rules had to be set. I began to type.

> Dear Rashana,
> I assume this is you again because I recognize the speech patterns and the heady concepts. But I was writing a book

and you interrupted my flow of ideas. Now it will take forever before I can get up the momentum to continue. I must say I'm not too happy about that.

Dearest Stuck in Time,
 That is an illusion that you have perpetrated upon yourself. The flow of ideas is a vibration and can be interrupted at any time and continued as soon as you can reconnect with the vibration of that particular idea or thought. But I don't wish to cause you unhappiness. I am more than willing to allow you to set the construct for this thing we will do together.
Love & Peace,
Rashana

Rashana,
 I still have no idea what you think we have to do together. Until that's clear to me, I don't know whether I'm even willing to agree to continue communicating with you.

All this talk of soul/spirit relationships was not only confusing, it was also infuriating. I had given up religion during the first year I worked in Pediatrics and saw what disease did to the kids. I was mad at God. Now, it was as though someone else had set up the plan for my life, and I didn't have any say it. *What about free will?* That was why I had become a writer. I hated bureaucracy, and I hated working for anyone else. I liked the freedom of working by and for myself. So, on any level, I had a real problem with the idea of destiny. It seemed to absolve the human being of any responsibility.

Rashana seemed to be able to read my mind.

> *Dear Only You,*
>
> *There is a truth I feel I must share with you in order to help you understand the work we must do together. You have never been by yourself, you have only been unaware or unconscious of the help you have been given. You have had several guides in your life to help you with your work. Remember the vision of Florence Nightingale you had before you "decided" to become a nurse? That was Eva, a High Spirit from the Core group of Healers, sent to remind you of your chosen path. She has been with you in all the most difficult periods of your life. I was unable to reach you at that time, because the vibration of your unhappiness over your lost love was so dense that I wasn't able to get through to you. But Eva is a passionate Spirit of the Highest Healing kind who enjoys working with the gifted but difficult souls on Earth. She volunteered to help reach you. Also, and this will most certainly come as a surprise to you, you have never worked for yourself, because our plan from the beginning was to work for the good of All.*
> *Love & Learning,*
> *Rashana*

My heart fluttered in my chest like a caged bird. *My vision of Florence Nightingale?* How did she know? That had happened so many years before. I was only twenty-four years old then. Until I went to nursing school and started studying the history of the profession, I didn't even know who the figure in the long amber wool cape holding the lantern had been.

At the time my marriage had been falling apart, my husband was gone, I was living in a strange house far from home, without food, heat or money, and I had two little kids depending on me to keep them alive. When that vision had first come to me, I was sure it was because of stress–either I was dreaming with my eyes open or going a little crazy.

I've had other visions since then that helped me with my life, but I always thought of them as projections of my own mind. If I ever imagined they were something more, it was something abstract, like iridescent arrows of Fate. Still, down deep, I never completely believed they were from anywhere outside myself. Now I was supposed to believe that it was Eva, a High Healing Spirit from the Core Group (whatever that is) who had been with me ever since?

> Dear Rashana,
>
> I'm going to have to get real with you now. I'm going to assume as much as I can that you are my higher self, not just some part of my own mind projecting itself onto my computer screen or some strange person who's just playing with me. I'm going to try to suspend my disbelief and take the fall into innocence. But I want you to know I don't completely trust this whole thing.

Dearest Marking Time or Marching in Place,

I am—though nothing is really separate—an aspect of the Light that exists in a realm other than your own. But I am also an aspect of yourself—not your mind, but your consciousness, because your consciousness is not a separate consciousness from All Consciousness. So I am both you and not you.

This communication is about relationships—about the interaction of spirit and soul. The expansion and evolution of consciousness in humankind from brain to mind to the subtler areas of soul, which also has a voice and an opinion, I might add. Anyone who has had what human livings consider a tragedy of any great proportion knows that the soul has a cry of its own. When one falls in love, one knows how deeply a soul can love, but who knows how a soul thinks and how it negotiates its relationship to its spirit, from whom it gets its map of the journey? Your higher self is the architect of your soul and is as important to know as the DNA of your physical body.

Living life's purpose is a big subject on your planet now, but who tells a human soul how to find that purpose? Well, your higher self or your spirit must help to communicate that to you. And you must be able to hear it.

In truth, we are both attributes of "God" or the All Knowledge. In other words, I'm both inside and outside because there truly is no difference.
Love in All,
Rashana

She was making my mind spin.

Dearest Rashana,
That's a pretty complicated concept. Could you make it any clearer? Could you tell me what this really has to do with me on earth at this time? I mean in practical terms?

My Dear Physical Aspect,
It has everything to do with you on Earth at this time. We wouldn't be communicating if there were no purpose. It is up to us to find the practicality of it. For one, I can be a great help in what you consider "Earthpoint Problems." I can offer advice that will help you reframe your belief system. In that way I can help you and others who wish to cut down on suffering. For when human livings understand some of the reasons for their "problems" or "challenges" they seem to be able to learn from them much more quickly. We can take this anywhere. In that way, as a spirit, I can also learn as you do. Two heads are better than one–even if one is not visible.
L&K
Rashana

Dear Rashana,
I don't mean to insult you, but I can talk to my friends if I need advice. How is this better?

Dearest One,

Do you have only one friend? Is not the advice of some friends more illuminating than others? Have you ever had a friend who advised something you hadn't even thought of? And haven't you found that friends who love you and know you intimately can be trusted to offer advice that is more helpful? Do some of your friends have more expanded vision than others? I am offering my love and friendship. Do you already have too many friends who love you unconditionally?
Luv,
Rashana

Dear Rashana,

Well, now that you've laid that right on the line, I have to ask what I have to offer you? If I accept the concept that you are my higher self, how is it possible that I can offer you anything?

Dearest Mine on Earth,

You can offer me a vision of your life and your planet as a human living sees, through physical eyes. You can offer me the understanding of "feelings" because Spirits do not experience emotions. We have common senses. I can learn more about relationships from you because, in the Light, All is One and therefore Earth is the place to practice "relationships." Also, I know nothing about separateness except what I've learned from my souls on Earth. And for me, in this moment, creative communications is something I wish to

know more about. I wish to know how my messages are interpreted by the human mind.
Love & All,
Rashana

I sat for a moment, just thinking. There had been other times when I might have welcomed just this kind of exploration. Whenever I was unhappy, I didn't mind change and I've always been interested in studies of human consciousness. But my life at that moment was going well. For the past several years I had been engaged to Mario Puzo, the author of the book, "*The Godfather*", as well as other good books, and we worked and played together while we traveled all over the world.

My life was pretty good. I felt I had a plan: I wanted to write some more books, finish getting my Master's in transpersonal psychology, enjoy my current love life, travel, spend time with my kids, learn more about my grandchildren and grow gracefully into wisdom and old age. My days seemed more than full. This communication from Rashana could be an opportunity, yes, but it certainly could herald greater growth—which to me always meant change. And when I was really doing okay, I didn't much like change.

> Dear Rashana,
> There's so much swirling around, my mind is spinning. I need to think about this. But if I decide to continue with you, how much of my time will it take?

Dear Near Sighted Soul,
   Put your mind to rest and let me suggest you check with your heart. We will, in any case,

continue our relationship. And if you feel you are running out of time, I must tell you that time, except on earth, is an illusion. I would like to accomplish this in this lifetime because of the opportunity for faster evolution in your soul and on your planet now, but if you prefer not to, we can wait until another life, in another space, in another place. I did want to give you a chance to choose to help your planet in the now.
Love and Loyalty,
Rashana

Dear Rashana,

Then, that's it? If I say I don't want to communicate with you at this time, you just go away and I never hear from you again?

My Own Soul,
Me, go away? I can't go away from you any more than you can go away from yourself. You are an aspect of me on Earth, and I am an aspect of you in the realm of the heavens. I can forego communicating with you in this way but I am always, and will always be, here to protect you and to aid you in your life. It is up to you whether I am up front with you, or work only behind the scenes.
Love, Rashana

Dear Rashana,

I give up! You win. We'll do whatever you want. What is it you want from me right now?

My Dearest Living Proof,
I sense some reluctance on your part to continue with the plans once made so I will allow you to tell me what it is that you need. How can I assist you in your life?
Rashana

Dear Rashana,
I have to earn a living, therefore I have to be able to write. I can't write if we are doing this every day. I need some peace and quiet. Can you help with that?

Dearest Accelerator,
You have already earned your living through what you have accomplished in this life, as well as in past lives. As far as peace and quiet, much of your discontent comes from the chattering of your own mind. I suggest that you center yourself each morning in order to meditate, or use a mantra for several minutes to connect with the Source of Universal Energy, which will bring great peace and a deep loving quiet. I will return when you have processed what we've asked of you.
Lovingly and Liltingly,
Rashana.

After that, months passed without any word from Rashana. It was winter, when I usually spend more time indoors meditating, exploring my inner space and pursuing new ideas for books and other writing. A lot had started to happen in my life that I wanted to brainstorm about, but Mario was involved in a new book so he wouldn't be able to hear me.

I decided to contact Rashana, just to see if she could help. I sent her an IM, but I didn't receive any response. I figured she had an attitude. After several days of not hearing from her, I wrote again.

> Dear Rashana,
> I have found it difficult to contact you in the last few days and I don't understand why.

> *Dear Soulie,*
> *I have as you know been decorating the skies with new and shiny stars. Every few eons the old stars get dusty or burn out and they have to be replaced. As a new spirit on the Creative realm, it is one of my jobs. I have even been awarded a golden wand. I'm now really looking at the creative aspects of myself, having mastered and integrated my warrior nature. It's quite magical.*

> Dear Rashana,
> Where does that leave me?

> *Dear Soulie,*
> *On Earth where you've always been. There was an agreement made before we started this whole thing at the beginning, that this was the time to do this. You as well as me, and so I'm just moving ahead as planned. Humans*

have short memories and so they forget plans once made but let me assure you that things are going exactly as we planned beforehand. Funny word. It's really before life at hand.

Dear Rashana,
After you finish redecorating the heavens, what then? What do you do and what do we do together?

Dearest Squashfeelings,
I do what spirits do. I don't have a complete idea just yet, for on the Creative Realm it's up to us to create what we'll do. Therefore I have to create a job and then make sure I fit the job description–which is no problem because I'll write a job description that requires a spirit of Light just like me. I'll let you know as soon as I finish beginning it.

As for us, well, here's the situation. We have to decide together. We can, of course, dance. And we can make visions that you can just sit and enjoy – very much better than pay TV.

You tune in and I'll show you what we can see together. Then we can be Mother Nature too, in a fashion, not the same as before. Not so much Italian overfeeding of other selves with emotion that belongs to you and fills a soul as fast as it fills a stomach. Makes one boggy and is not good for soul health. I want to have lighter time on earth with you.

Too many lifetimes filled with suffering have made it difficult for me to laugh as lightly as a spirit should and we really must consider my wishes as well. I will, as always, respect your choice of what you wish to do, but beautiful is not as trivial as you seem to think it is. If everyone took on so heavy an incarnation at all times, no one would volunteer to come to earth for lessons. Also it pains my spirit compassion to watch you struggle with such important matters all the lifetimes. It sets you and me out of balance. That too is a form of stuckness.

The Thirteenth Master has it in hand – His and Her hands. No need to feel it's always in your/our hand. He/She is quite the most wonderful and fair and compassionate and balanced of All so we must allow our plan to flow.

Stop asking for such heavy work, you'll burn yourself out. Then you keep dying too quickly and learn no lessons of good old age, of which you have far too little experience.

I am looking forward to your wrinkles. In all our incarnations, we have not had great-grandchildren. Is that not in itself a certain enough sadness for you?

Anyway we have much to contribute if you can help to rid yourself of the notion that only your suffering is worthwhile. Your laughter is quite a nice sound and your smile is quite a beautiful one. Sometimes other souls hunger for the look of a smile that has not the sad eyes of too many burdens beneath.

In the meantime I will return to my creations and anytime you wish to contact me you can just.

With starry eyes and huge smiles, I remain Yours,
Rashana

※

After that, I was writing and Rashana was writing back pretty consistently. But now I was getting worried. I was spending a lot of time writing, communicating with a part of myself I didn't even know existed until just a short time before.

In my current reality on earth, I had run into a masked burglar at Mario's house in the middle of the night. One of my concerns was that it didn't frighten me at the time, which I thought was strange, so I wanted to be sure that nothing was going on behind the scenes that was altering my consciousness.

I figured it was time to see a shrink. Throughout my life, whenever I felt I needed help with growth and change, I visited a therapist to help me grow in a healthier way. Now, I felt I needed a second opinion about all that was happening, or maybe a third. I had mine and Rashana's, but maybe it would be a good thing to get the known out of the way before delving more deeply into the unknown. It was obvious, even to me, that once you had more friends without bodies than with, something odd was happening.

I'd spent years studying the psychology and physiology of the brain while I was researching my second book, "Rusty's Story," and I knew how much we didn't know. Still, I figured maybe in the same way Freud changed our knowledge of anatomy when he discovered that the mind was different from the brain, Spirit was moving into the unchartered territory of my brain and opening new circuits which were making me more aware. I knew I should at least rule out a few things.

The only good therapist I knew and trusted was a Jungian analyst, Dr. Gerry Canon. That very afternoon, I called and made an appointment. She scheduled me for the following day.

I was relieved. Even though I believed in inner journeys, it couldn't hurt to have someone in the outside world help map the way.

As I walked into her office, I was wondering how to explain what had been going on. She greeted me with a handshake and a smile.

"How have you been?" she asked, warmly.

While I had been sitting in the car waiting for my appointment, I read through my journal notes and tried to figure out what I was going to say. But as soon as we sat down in her office, I just thrust the papers at her and said, "Here. Could you tell me what you think?"

It took her about fifteen minutes to read through them. Then she looked up and said, "Sounds like good advice."

"Am I making it up?" I asked her. "Is it my imagination, am I a multiple, or is Rashana real?"

"What's imagination?" she asked. "What's real? But no, you're not a multiple. You have too much ego integrity. None of this is going on without your knowledge."

"You don't understand," I tried to explain. "Something happened a couple of months ago. One night when I was sleeping over Mario's, I ran straight into a burglar who robbed us blind. Well, not exactly blind, but he did take a lot of money that Mario had given me to buy Christmas presents. He took it right out of my pocketbook as I was sleeping, and that pocketbook was leaning against the bed not two inches from my nose."

"That must have frightened you," she said.

"Not really," I said, "It's strange. He didn't even wake me up, though I'm a really light sleeper. Although the aftermath was scary as all hell because I didn't understand how that could happen.

"I woke up at 4:03 am because I dreamed someone had tapped my shoulder. But Mario was still asleep so I got up to go to the bathroom. When I passed Mario's study, there was this big guy standing in the doorway. Really big, and he was dressed in black, wearing a mask, except for a brown sweater. Because of the mask, I could only see the whites of his eyes but he was carrying one of those long black flashlights in his right hand. He had black gloves on too, and black sneakers."

"Why weren't you frightened?" she asked.

"Haven't got a clue. My mind was doing a funny thing. He seemed familiar to me. All I could do was smile as I was thinking, 'What are you doing in that getup?'"

"Who did you think he was?" she asked.

"Now this is even funnier. I had been working on a paper about Buddhism for a course in transpersonal psychology. I had fallen asleep thinking about the Buddha sitting under the Bodhi tree while all the faces of death and desire danced before him. But no matter what he saw, he sat, unmoving. No matter how frightening or tempting the visions, he sat still. Finally after he sat long enough, he saw they were illusions, and well, that's when he reached enlightenment."

"What did that have to do with this situation?" she asked simply. "Can you explain it?"

"Well, that's why I stood fast. I mean, my whole life I prayed for enlightenment. At the time it made sense to me though now as I say it, it doesn't really. But that's because I haven't told you the missing piece. That night Mario and I were going over the screenplay he had written for the next *Godfather* movie. In one scene, two masked burglars dressed in black broke into the apartment of Vincent Mancini, Sonny's son. Vincent wakes up, walks into the hall with his tall, blond, gorgeous girlfriend behind him. One of the burglars grabs her, puts a knife to her throat, and threatens to kill her if Vincent doesn't hand over the money. But Vincent just laughs and says, 'Go ahead.'"

"And?" Dr. Canon, asked, confused.

"The reason that sticks in my mind is that Mario couldn't stop laughing, and I didn't get the humor in it. When I asked what was funny about it, Mario explained that even though Vincent was a hotheaded guy, he was a likeable guy and women still saw him as a sort of honorable knight, so they wouldn't expect him to react like that. But I still didn't get it. I figured it was a guy thing. So both the Buddha and the Godfather's grandson, Vincent, were on my mind when I fell asleep that night."

"Okay," she said, concentrating hard.

"Well, when I saw the burglar, I thought 'Oh I get it. The Buddhists believe that thought makes form. Then

I had another lightbulb moment. It must be a test, I thought, a contemporary version of the Buddha's test of discrimination. But something struck me as a little off. Because I was a nurse, my face of death would never have been a grade B thug in the Godfather's house. My face of death would have been disease."

"Can you remember what happened next?" she asked.

"I saw what looked like a circle of light around this guy's feet. Then I swear I heard someone say, 'It's a Tai Chi circle,' so I knew not to step into it. Suddenly, while I'm standing fast, my hands flying because I'm Italian so I talk with my hands and I think with them too, this guy bows like a prince, backs away, and closes the door. Now, that's when I panicked! Shit! Shit! Shit! I thought. There are no closed doors on the path of enlightenment! This must be the last scene from *The Godfather*, and I'm in the wrong movie. That's when I woke Mario up."

"How did he react?" she asked.

"Well, he jumped right out of bed, grabbed on to the handle of the door to hold it closed, and told me to call the cops. By that time, my realities were so mixed up that I wasn't sure of anything, so I told him I'd rather wait until we were sure there really was a burglar in his study. That's when he asked me to go downstairs and get a big carving knife, and he'd keep holding the door closed."

"And you went?" she asked, trying to hide her amusement.

"I did," I said, laughing. "And when I came upstairs holding two huge knives, Mario said, 'Two? What for? Why two?' I said, 'Hey, you didn't see how big he was. If he skewers you, I don't want to be defenseless.'

"Mario laughed so hard that he let go of the door and it flew open. That's when we could see that drawers had been pulled out of his desk and tossed on the couches, and everything was scattered all over the floor in his study. But by then the burglar was gone, and a cold wind was blowing through the open sliding doors to the balcony."

"That must have frightened you," she said.

"It should have," I told her. "But it really didn't. Whether that's shock or not, I don't know, but I never would have guessed I'd react that way."

"Why do you think you did?" she asked.

I pointed to the papers on her lap, my notes about my experience. "I could swear someone woke me up. But I guess because I thought I knew him, it kept me from being afraid and probably saved my life." I took a deep breath before I asked, "So do you think I've lost my mind? You can tell me. Am I crazy?"

"Not at all," she said. "You've read about Jung's archetypes and the collective unconscious. But have you ever read Stan Grof's books on spiritual emergence? There have been some other books written by Christina Grof and some anecdotal accounts as well. You should read them, and then we'll talk again."

"Maybe I'll go have a physical too, just to be sure."

"Good idea," she said. "Call if you need me."

✺

The following day I went to my regular doctor for a physical. I went through my whole story again and the doctor, who was also a friend, told me I'd been working too hard, and that I should go home and get some rest. I decided to check with another friend of mine who was a neurologist. He also listened to my story, and then ordered an EEG and an MRI.

That afternoon, I went to the radiology lab and naively climbed into the MRI machine. Once they wheeled me into the huge metal tube I couldn't bear the feeling of claustrophobia. I felt as though I'd been buried alive, and I swear I could feel my molecules moving around. I figured exploratory brain surgery would be better.

After the neurologist had read the EEG report, he seemed surprised that it showed mostly delta and theta waves. He explained that was not exactly normal for a waking state. When I asked what it meant, he reassured me it didn't indicate any kind of "significant" damage. He did acknowledge "something happened" but he didn't feel it was a danger at the moment. He wanted to follow up with another EEG in a few weeks, and I promised I would. He also suggested that he could medicate me to make a repeat MRI more "comfortable." I refused.

During the next week on the advice of my friend Dee Krieger, a professor at NYU who developed and taught Therapeutic Touch, I went upstate to visit Dora Kunz, a well-known New Age healer, to see what she felt. All she did after walking around and assessing my energy "field" was laugh and say, "Well, we wouldn't consider this a normal brain." Her expression reassured me and her laughter relaxed me. Besides, no matter what anyone found, I wasn't about to let a surgeon into my brain to probe around.

☙❦☙

During the following months, I started to meditate regularly, listen to tapes on enlightenment, and read everything I could find on shamanism, spiritual growth and emergence. In the meantime, I kept writing to Rashana.

> Dear Rashana,
> I am glad to find out that losing my mind didn't mean I was losing myself, but I am concerned about all the "things" I've been seeing. Why all the scary visions lately?

> *Dear Silliness,*
> *Don't accept, absolutely refuse all images of a fearful nature. For protection, seal yourself with wide impermeable slabs of red, green, and yellow luminescence, and flash the Light of your heart near any negative vision. The Light blinds whoever or whatever is not of it. Fill your thoughts with good. Bagavid Gita is a fine book to know now. Read twenty. Keep away from all fear of death without transition books. Transformation books would be fine, though limited in their application for now. Forget the Catholic bible or anything that inspires fear. Read earth books. You know you're unlimited, read how others on your plane deal with the limits and you will understand better during this time. Eat greens. Drink water.*
> *Eva will begin to shower you with colors two times each day. Stop smoking one half hour before to make communication easier with us at that time. I must say you certainly*

can help choke the negatives with all the smoking you've been doing. That will stop soon. The headache pain is to distract you from reading. Insist on going on. Don't let this delay you. Gay Luce is fine. Ram Dass is of course good. All is going well–as we expected.

Dear Rashana,
 It is funny for me to think of my spirit as being as obsessive as I am. I never thought of spirit as anything but completely balanced–perfect in a way, I guess. Now I see our problem much more clearly. I'd like to present it to you and maybe you could share some of your spirit insight as I offer my soul vision.
 I'll grant that I probably helped exhaust you while I was running around trying to stamp death and disease out of the Western hemisphere during all those years of nursing. Especially since death and disease are as much a part of earth life as stars are a part of the heavens. But then it occurs to me that in your passion to do creative heavenly spirit things, you were doing the same thing by redecorating the heavens and cleaning up the stars. I figured God would take care of death and disease *and* replacing the stars if we would get on with what we wanted to do.
 Saving souls? I know we can't do that together because you want to do only "beautiful" now that you're off the

warrior realm. Besides I finally understand that each soul must save itself.

Eva, High spirit from the Core group, has offered to help me as a Hopeful Healer. So you're off the hook in case you don't want to be part of the New World healer thing, which is what I've decided I'd like to do.

I do wonder if you are willing to write a few articles with me that involve some healing concepts that are quite beautiful. It would fill my need to do something essential during this incarnation. We could do it, as you suggested, more in a nurturing way than a warrior way, and still get our point across. Would you be willing to do that?

Dearest Partner in Comfort,

It has been brought to my attention at Core Counsel that I have been a little too enthusiastic about making a contribution to the Creative realms. I have been informed by the Lightest Luminaries that Creative existed before I got there and would continue after I move on which of course it has already been decided I will. Spirits must learn and grow as well as souls and that's exactly what I've been doing. I'd like to congratulate you for all your insights. I would, of course, like to take credit for some of them but actually I've been too busy trying to adjust to my new circumstance to be of much help to you.

Therefore I had asked Eva to help and because it had already been decided, she accepted before we ever made a move. She has done marvelous work with your soul in this time. I had almost despaired of ever getting through your rational mind to your heart in order for you to be able to see things clearly.

By the way, spirit needs to be left to do spirit things sometimes without having to worry about soul things. Could you just seek and find and try some things on your own and then we will help pick up the pieces if any fall, which is not so likely. You do not have to communicate constantly with spirit. Spirit always knows what is going on and taking time out of your day to sit for too many hours trying to reach us when we are already there is a waste of what human livings call time. At any rate, you are wasting yourself when you do it. We are there if you need us. Did Eva not wake you for the soul encounter with the burglar? We chose someone from a past life you knew well, so as not to frighten you too much.

Now to answer the question you asked of me. I, of course, would be willing to write with you. Fiction or nonfiction, your call.

Dear Rashana,
So that's it? We're set? From now on we're on track then?

My Goodness,
We are just beginning again. Your soul is very new in its own way now and I would

like to suggest that you fill it with happy and sunshine things. A leaf or two of the outside world couldn't hurt, and a new leaf in a new book would truly lighten and happy me up. Let's fill it with beautiful things.

I would like to suggest that it would serve you not to be so compulsive about even the things that you feel you "need" to do. I wish also to continue to write the fiction we began, the one called "The Azurite" I may tell you I am enjoying this new realm but can often be affected by what you do, so I need to remind you of our connection.

Eva is doing well with your healing with colors, and though you will never be as "sharp" as you were before, you will certainly accomplish more balance. Rational mind was causing quite a tilt. Heart vision will allow you to speak directly to others who can hear the truth of words spoken straight from the heart.

In the space provided please eat, rest, read and be happy. Things are looking up, up, up, so up that soon we will feel free as a balloon. Heartfully Yours, Rashana

One afternoon the following week, I was feeling bombarded by sensory impressions—my head and body felt battered by all the sights, sounds and colors in my world. At first I thought it was just a migraine, but when it wouldn't let up, I decided to write to Eva so as not to bother Rashana with my healing questions.

To tell the truth, the last few days my senses had become so acute that even my skin was sensitive to any small breeze. I could hear leaves blowing across my driveway at night, and smell flowers from the yard across the street as though someone was sitting next to me wearing too much perfume. It occurred to me that I had always thought of the brain as an information gatherer, but I had underestimated how important a part it played as a gatekeeper. In blocking some of the sensory information that filled the space around me, it allowed me to process that information without overloading my senses. For the first time I really understood how people who are labeled "mentally ill" or "autistic" must feel. That constant assault on one's senses certainly could drive a person crazy. Until then, I never realized how completely the "reality" of my three-dimensional world depended on a shift in gestalt. Now all of life and other space seemed painted on a single canvas. I swear it looked like an oil painting by Pieter Bruegel, The Elder.

Rashana was more comfortable with joy and beauty than with my questions about healing, so whenever I asked about healing, Rashana began to speak about beauty. She insisted that truth and beauty were healing. And that in the final event truth breaks into beauty and creativity. So I found it easier to talk to Eva about my current concerns.

Whenever I imagined Eva, or called to her, I saw a swirling mix of lavender and green—alive and moving. I had never seen a color like it on earth. Also, with Eva, I had impressions of thought, but not as many words or concepts as I could hear with Rashana. I was curious to see if Eva would respond in words if I wrote. So I sat, closed my eyes and put my fingers on the keyboard.

Dear Eva,

I feel really out of touch with so many of the people I was close to before this brain shift, and have lost so much faith in most of society's systems, like medicine, that I used to believe in, I don't know where to stand. I know I don't want to work in hospitals any longer, because I don't really see them as healing now. I want to do a transition book from the old paradigm of medicine to a New World model of hopeful healing. What do you feel about helping me as long as Rashana doesn't want to?

Dearest Top Flight Student,

I want to first reassure you that your healing is going quite the way it should. I feel it is important for you to understand that if one is meant to be healed, healing will occur by any means that is chosen—alternative or traditional means. The most important element in your understanding is that healing travels from spirit down through the emotional body to physical body. And sometimes the healing of the physical body is not within a human being's purpose.

In reference to being out of touch with friends and others, you must understand that each growth spurt brings change. Certainly there are times of difficulty, but is that not as we showed it should be? Obstacles, even in the form of our other selves, are good, and must be compromised with.

> *Spirit wishes Carol to know that Rashana is one of the fullest Light, and yet she is one who felt great responsibility to have others see the light of her love. We did assure her often that other high spirits of Light were here, there, and everywhere, but in her zeal she often tried to accomplish at once what All had accepted before as time enough. At any rate she is doing so well now that she will be a great help in the beauty side, the softer side, of your nature. She is a far-tuned learner and so she is often a little ahead of herself, which can on occasion cause you to lose some balance. I suggest for your own good that you try to balance her spirit nature and your soul nature which will be wonderful for both realms. Of course, All will help accomplish such a task.*
> *Light and Love,*
> *Eva*

I was really relieved that each of my spirits seemed to have a place and a purpose in my life. Rashana could help bring beauty and joy into my soul and help me with my creative writing, and Eva was willing to help me with a new model of healing. For the first time in a long time, I felt that as a soul, I really did have free will.

During the past weeks, I had noticed a difference in my relationship with Rashana. She did seem a little harder to reach, a little farther away from me. I wondered what was up. So I sat and wrote.

> Rashana,
> My head is clearing up a bit and so I'm feeling better. Still, this new way of

functioning, from heart, without my Italian guilt or sense of responsibility, leaves me a little uncertain. When my soul felt really burdened, I knew how most others felt. Now that I feel freer and you want to do only "beautiful," I'm feeling sort of separate from most people and not too close to you. What's up?

Dearest Lead Weight of the Most Loving Kind,
We have to come to some agreement with ourselves and not teeter like this. I will consider your need to do what your soul feels is essential and allow a few burdens if you must have them, but I would like you to consider my need of physical beauty, sunshine, trees, sky and fun-loving living as well. In that way we may accomplish some balance.

I too have been missing our close association and yet I was becoming too heavy for a spirit of my Light and so we had to be stretched. You will effect more of what we want to do in a lighter softer way now because I am able to help as never before. Have you not heard of a battered spirit?

Well, spending all that time, or whatever we call it, trying to right the wrongs of the world which were not really wrong from my vantage point, was becoming impossible for me. I had gotten truly fond of our partnership in this life and was hoping you would choose to stay as promised before hand but in no way could we continue in the way we were going. That is when Eva offered to help. Eva looks forward to the challenge of working with the gifted but difficult students. She will of course help in any way she can if we ask. The Thirteenth Master has been overlooking all and is laughing with pleasure and fun. We are all doing so well in this New World. And He/She is so pleased with this whole thought that we have been blessed in the highest sense.

Lighten up my little star so we can decorate the heavens with ourselves and appreciate the sunshine and starshine on earth.
Love In Light,
Rashana

During the following weeks I was finding it almost impossible to pick up a book, though one of my greatest enjoyments before this time had been reading. Now I couldn't hold a thought for as long as it took to tell it to someone else. To keep myself from panicking, I practiced single-minded focus and living in the "now." Which for me, at that time, was the only thing that seemed to exist.

I stopped reading the newspaper because it seemed senseless to pay for such bad news. I thought one of my nutty friends was trying to trick me by buying those made-up dailies at an amusement park or carnival and having it delivered to me–taking a "pretend" newspaper with horrifying headlines and substituting it for the real one. The only things I could read without being petrified were the ads.

I knew something was definitely wrong when I found myself in tears and completely overwhelmed by watching the evening news on TV. Wars, natural disasters and crime filled the airwaves and actually made me feel seasick. The broadcaster's voice would reverberate in my ears, making me dizzy.

Something was happening to me. I had never before been so sensitive, been such a sissy, is what I thought. But during that time, I couldn't believe that we, as human beings, would act toward each other in such hurtful and negative ways. Besides, I began to disbelieve most of what I read or heard. Everything sounded like lies to me. I didn't know what was happening but I began to stay home more than usual, and even refused to drive for a while. I was beginning to feel as though I had dropped out of the human race and I seriously began to worry about my capacity to ever feel "normal" again.

Then one night I got a call from Mario, and all he said was, "Come over, I set myself on fire...but I'm okay."

The following morning the first thing I did was sit at my computer and write to Rashana.

> Rashana,
>
> Mario set himself afire last night while he was cooking, burned his bathrobe and caught his hair on fire but never burned any skin. How is that possible? Even more miraculous, after being afraid to drive or even go out for the last month, as soon as he called, I jumped into the car and raced right over to his house without a moment's hesitation. So at least I still have a heart and a wish or need to help. It kept me from feeling I was a monster, anyway. Seemed pretty

funny when I thought about it, all of it. Could you help clear up the matter and tell me its meaning?

Dearest Fire Fighter of the Highest Kind,
    There was a spirit from this Mario's past who blew out the fire like she blew out the candles on his birthday cake. We thought we had shown how people could still survive their lives without your help. It was fun to know you got there too late to do anything but help in a consoling way. Cut hair, this is good. Like Delilah. Notice? Watch that you don't get sucked into playing the new story of "you took my strength." He will play the funniest games with you to sharpen your wit. Don't play halfway but truly understand that this is play of the highest kind.
    I am about ready to begin the material we signed on to do. Please allot some special time to write this fiction. I am aware that you have been wanting to write the truth about the healing journey but I hope you understand I can not help with that at this point. Eva of course is more than willing to.
Love in Light,
Rashana the Rainbow

Dear Rashana,
    Well, my head's still a little fuzzy but I think it's because I've been doing a little too much on the heavy side. I do know now that there are energy exchanges

between people both positive and negative that can effect us physically. Fear is a big negative–it drains energy. I spent too much time at the hospital today, visiting one of my good friends and her family, talking to lots of people and trying to reassure them about her dying.

For the past couple of weeks, I guess I've been more involved in other peoples' lives and not enough in my own. The book contract for the healing book came in and I signed it, so I'm on my way to working again. But it's still pretty cold out and it's hard for me to enjoy the beauty of nature when I dislike the cold so much.

I must admit I feel less creative when you're not involved in what I'm doing. I was wondering how things were going for you? I want to start a small publishing house for all our beautiful books and the healing books I do with Eva. What do you think about calling it Star Water Press?

Dearest My Noir Mystic in Society,

Sorry about the pun. You know that all mystical work is major especially in society today, but you also know by black (noir) I mean "seeing power," not negativity. It was just too funny to let go.

As for us, I'm sort of pleased at the way things are going. Star Water Press is a beautiful concept. I finally understand your need to be essential–a need not shared by spirit at All, because it's so apparent—but sometimes a soul feels the necessity to help accomplish what is already accomplished. I forgot that need until you reminded me strongly that sometimes a beautiful life is not enough.

Eva has been doing well with your healing still. Hopefully you'll begin to focus on the paradigm that allows letting go: letting go of all restrictions, of rational mind, of old beliefs, of suffering. Heart is a good place to function from. It has a lighter brighter sight. Most of rational mind is filled with weeds and flowers planted by others. Your origins are and have always been your heart. Soul mind retains what is necessary and rational mind carries all the extra baggage. How can you be free and light with all you were carrying? That doesn't even seem a rational choice. But then it seems that human livings are always crying over spilled baggage even when there is earth, sea, sky, life and other beautiful sights to enjoy.

How am I? That was nice of you to ask. I've still been trying to compile a list of things for us to do in this life that are beautiful. The list was quite long so in order to make an allowance for your essential soul work to honor your sufferings, I had to balance my list of only the beautiful. I think our attitude of positiveness—if we can curb our impatience and our need to get things done—will allow us to have quite a lovely life on earth. Our laugh itself will be a healing sound and our bright sunny nature will surprise many and also please you and me.

I do hate to haunt, it is not appropriate for a spirit of my nature, but the smoking too much is making our communication more difficult. It tires you while you are adjusting to a new vibration. Cut back just a bit to see how you feel. I don't mind the spirit of the animals you eat, your spirit nature and mine can transform them with love into evolution for our animal friends.

I think it is time for us to start the fiction material. Set aside at least an hour each day and I will show you what we can do together. I have to accomplish the greater part of this job description for Hopeful Healing based on the Truth and Beauty aspects in the next few days so I will go now. Get moving, excuse me, please go forward at your leisure with things that make you happiest and that will help me along. I'm looking forward...
Love and Lightning
Lighter Love,
Rashana

Everyone else seemed to be going about business as usual, not at all aware of the radical change in direction my consciousness had taken. I still couldn't read, or remember, and I couldn't come up with anything I really wanted to write about.

Several times over the next weeks when I was confused or upset, I found myself racing over to my computer to write. Sometimes to Eva, other times to Rashana. The very act of that communication seemed to ground me.

Dearest Eva,
 Can you shed any light on whether or not there's something wrong with my brain, and why it refuses to work in the ways it used to? And do you think I should have another EEG or a CAT scan to make certain nothing physical is going on?

Dearest Star Bright,
 It's no matter and of no consequence. One can be a halfwit with a full brain and one can be a full wit with a half brain.

Dear Eva,
 That's funny. But is this condition temporary?

Dearest Long Term Seer,
 All conditions are temporary. This particular one is more temporary than most because you have finally learned what we had been trying to teach for years: to see with your heart. It is now of the utmost importance that you don't try to return to functioning as before. It's of no gain and certainly not of a healing mode. Whether you have been fortunate enough to manifest such an easy path toward enlightenment is yet to be discovered. Because of science and technology today, you may have a peek at human possibilities if you care to, but at any rate whatever has been accomplished by All thus far has only to be recognized. Can't you see that?

Dear Eva,
Why are you not signing your name any longer? Am I just meant to know who you are?

Dearest Pandemonium,
I am All in One, as are many other Core Healers. If you wish for me to state it again and again, then I may, but I wish to explain that when I call myself Eva, there is a false distinction or a limit being imposed on both of us. I am, as you know and can feel in your heart and your hands, a healer of the highest kind. All of us have been with you always in all ways.

Dearest Eva,
Why call me pandemonium? Why that name?

Dearest May Flower,
I am referring to a paradigm of learning but also to the clanking of the mind you've sworn you've lost. Have some belief in the knowledge that everything will work out the way it will and then you can quiet your soul mind and be more aware of the moment. I had hoped that in your discoveries, you could move away from a science way of thinking. Yet, maybe the time is not completely right. You may feel comfort in the cause you have chosen to perpetuate if that is where you are going. I'm not trying to be unkind. It may be a necessary evil at this time. No pun in-

tended. You, as a soul, may understand what soul earth needs now to make that jump into Hopeful Healing, yet if we continue to see science and medicine as a mecca, we will slow down the process of learning. Is seeing believing and will you then believe in your power or ours?

Dearest Eva,
You are confusing me. I thought you asked if I wanted to see the vision and now you ask why?

*Dearest Carrot,
I want to help you see from all points so as to make your choice more choiceful. There may be a period of transition that is needed for you to fully trust and acknowledge what you already know. I'm trying to help you along in the same hard-muscle way that medicine does. We are following a pattern that you seem used to. I hope it helps in your decision.*

Dear Rashana,
I'm really getting aggravated with myself and therefore with you as well. I like working with Eva but I want to work with you too. Could you help make things a little clearer?

*Dearest Pain in the Cosmos,
We're working on freedom. You, as a human living, have to take some responsibility for soul choice. I cannot do your work and mine.*

It wouldn't be appropriate even if we had time, which on this plane we don't.
  Now I will try to help clear things up. I want to do creative fiction. On your plane, they see it as fiction, but here it is fact. So it is purely what you would call a marketing decision. Call it what you like, but let's do it first. You haven't even tried to write anything creative with my help so far, except this notebook of your transformation. So that's a start, but what are you going to do in the other moments of your life? Is that the question? Okay, maybe I can help here too.
  I would like to walk on the beach, the weather is getting quite lovely. I would like to do some physical things with you. You cannot transcend an experience unless you have had it. In this lifetime, you cannot say that you have seen your world. It is my job now to see that you do creative things, like live. You cannot die before you've lived, and so please put your heart to living fully. Now Eva is on the realm of very valuable sight and healing. She has offered too many times already to help you do whatever you wish.
  You may do everything a day can hold but not by sitting down to think about what that is. Just start. Do anything. You will then at least have accomplished something besides deciding what to do. Your soul mind is freezing because you have not warmed it with the light of day or the sun.
  You may see in time, but in the space between, you must redo some new things, see

some new sights, and do some writing. You must also have some fun.

I know that seems a ridiculous thing to impose upon a soul, but if you are intending to stay alive, there has to be a reason. You've gotten stuck in old age thinking. This is the New World, where laughter is healing and so is dancing and fooling around. Stop being so tentative about everything. How many mistakes do you think can't be undone? There is Justice, as you have seen and now we're looking at Truth. Are you finding out that human livings don't want freedom? That in some funny way they are not up to "no limits"? Are you finding that they need the cages they build in order to feel a false safety?

Or do you think this is only you? Well then, try breaking out yourself and find what the potentials are. How can you even hope to help heal others if you can't go far enough in healing yourself? Be one, be All, but Be, and try to enjoy it. The time for pain is over. You are not meant to make an example of yourself in sickness, but rather in beauty.

Dear Rashana,
I am truly trying to understand. But I would like to know why, even when I understand that this brain shift is a gift because it's lifted me from the boundaries of my rational mind, it still feels like a loss?

My Very Darling Monkey,
Human livings see change as loss. As I have said, in order to transcend anything,

you must experience it first. So, you are now experiencing loss, then you will transcend it and find it has been a gift. It's all in the way of looking at things.

You can speak, you can walk, you can write, and when you meditate or sleep, your mind is empty and so you can rest as you never could before. No thoughts, no worries. That's an add, not a loss, isn't it? You can now speak the truth of your heart because you cannot manipulate the truth into lies with your rational mind. You're on a Truth realm now, so that's at least adaptive if not an add. You can feel us, you can feel your body, you can see nature as never before. Is that too not an add? You have long hours of freedom to read, even if you do not remember with your rational mind. What is necessary is being recorded in your soul mind, and you can play as you wish. You can listen to music, you can dance now, you can drive, you can cook, you can make love and you can make dreams even when you are awake. Does this not seem also like an add? Have we forgotten something that you truly wanted?

Dear Rashana,

All you say makes perfect sense and yet the loss of my rational mind makes me feel insecure and less confident. I'm not sure what I can do now. Also, I was a nurse and a writer before and most of what drove me was the fight for justice and the need to help others break down a system I knew was inhumane and not healing. Now I'm not sure what I should be doing.

Dearest Density of Many Matters,
You should be doing whatever you want to be doing. The old system was very appropriate for the warrior we were. In this moment the breakdown is appropriate in order for us to break through and move on to a nurturing mother nature and create something humane and healing. We can now be creative in how we do that. I am able to help with laughing fun matters and Eva is more than willing to help with a new model for healing. You have at least two soul purposes, or one with at least a dual purpose.

You have help in both fiction and nonfiction writing and you already have two contracts in the earth world to fulfill.

You have spring to explore, with trees and sun and beaches. Your body is intact, even more whole than before with only a part of the mind you constructed, or prefabricated, gone. You may rebuild with newer concepts. Use your other senses. Mind is often nonsense, and so all we removed was the nonsense in order to help you make sense of your world.

We are getting to the space of having to move. You may come along or you may sit until winter again. In the meantime, life and spirit and seasons and space time will continue as predetermined and if you do not decide the sweep of it, All will take you along to where you should be anyway. So be determined

in your adventure and we will continue as planned. By the way, you are doing quite well in your transition. I will await your full awakening and am here, there and everywhere as well. Shine on my little one.
Love and Light,
Rashana

One night my granddaughter, Ashley, Teri's sixteen-month-old, passed out and had to be taken to the Emergency Room. That was a more difficult situation than it would normally be because Teri's first son, Greggy, had died of SIDS. So, while Teri was at the hospital, I was filled with anxiety.

Dearest Rashana,
As you know, Ashley stopped breathing and turned blue. They're taking her to the hospital for testing. Can you shed any light on this for me?

Dearest Concerned Parent,
Of Teri, we mean. Ashley did not stop breathing. She just took a break. Why? Because she was in a temper and also sometimes a little in space which is not unusual for children of her nature. She is not going anywhere else for good. She will come back fine each time. Now, the problem, as you call it? That has to be determined on a spirit level of learning by the child and her parents. It is all healing and your child will learn much by it. The child Ashley has a very well-developed right brain, creative in its manifestations.

> *What does that mean? She is a beautiful sight and she will grow out of this way of manifesting and all will have grown so much. She has a very strong will and decided to show her parents in a very creative way what they must learn about trust. She was demonstrating for them the difference between the nature of her love for her parents and that of her brother, Gregory's. That is all. Evaluate it for yourself when you see the child. And relax.*
> *Love,*
> *Rashana at rest*

Sure enough, when Teri called later that night she told me the pediatrician said that she had both good news and bad news. The good news is that Ashley was perfectly fine, she had really good breath sounds and nothing showed up on the EEG. The bad news was that she had a really bad temper.

❦

The following morning, when I woke up, I decided to meditate to center myself, cover myself with Eva's colors for healing and to ask her some questions. I figured if I could get a ritual to do each morning, the rest of my day would be less confusing. As it was, my mind was full of creative ideas but very few of them were grounded in the "reality" I was now living.

> Dear Eva,
> Why is it that I feel so off balance, not quite dizzy but not quite focused, and it takes much longer to accomplish any-

thing concrete I need to do? I'd like to trust that everything will be alright but I keep feeling exhausted and as though I'm just on the edge of "losing it."

Oh My Dear,
　　This is Eva, and I wish to explain that this test can only be accomplished if you trust in the honor and integrity of your spirit guides. You do not need to understand to accept. Each day keep a journal of what you are doing, then some form or physical exercise for a half hour each morning. I know this will be difficult but two walks around the block in the next week. If you wish to speed your soul growth, you must get moving. I will help with insights at this time. Go alone. Rashana will watch over you so no need to fear anything, she is a match for anyone. Belief plays an important part here. Have you decided not to do some of the plans of freedom, or healing or writing? Is it more than too much for you now? Think about what you wish to give and get in life and then begin to plan so that it works in the best way. We are all here and all rooting for you. It is coming to a time where life is easier and you will have all the energy you need. Just sit and place your fingers on the keys and we will do the rest.
　　Rashana will return now, please be kind to each other and play together.
Healing Pink,
Eva

Dearest Feather Brain,

I have quite a hard time accepting that I must consider telling you what we've planned but I know Eva is right in her All Wise ways. I will do anything beautiful with you and I thank you for the cloud dancing this morning. I would like more of that. I was writing the next chapter of our life and it's so funny that you will cry with happy tears when you live it. I love to talk with you when you are rushing ahead with "essential work" for that is the essence of our relationship. Still, a lighter look will help our advance.

As soon as you are willing to meditate more often, I will show you other visions. Everything is coming along in a fine way, as good as we expected from All, and we are pleased. The weather is balmy and I would have liked a walk but maybe next time. I'll sign off for now. Your suffering wears me out as much as it does you. I will take a break and have some angel fuzz rejuvenation.
Love as always, and Light as well.
Rashana

Just then, like a streaming movie, a vision of a pretty young girl who looked like a Disney fairy flashed before my eyes. She was wearing a long blue cotton dress, ballerina shoes, and hopping from one cloud to another. I zoomed in closer so I could see her face. She was truly adorable, with a small turned up nose and a great smile. I was wondering who she was but almost immediately, it dawned on me. "Rashana?" I thought. "Is this you?"

When she turned toward me and winked, I knew.

"What are you doing with long blond hair?" I asked. "I thought you would look more like me."

"I was just practicing my vision-tossing technique," she said. "And it worked quite well, don't you think?"

"I can't believe the blond hair," I said.

Rashana was sipping something that I was certain was angel fuzz, because instead of bubbles I could see little halos floating around inside a glass she now held in her hand. Before I could say anything, she winked one more time and was gone.

❧

That winter Mario and I went to Malibu and stayed in Burgess Meredith's house on the beach, as we had done each year since 1981.

There, I had several months of peace and quiet with no responsibility, so I could read and write while looking out over the Pacific Ocean. But of course, after the first month, I got obsessed again, and worked most of the time. I edited and transcribed many of the screenplays and books Mario was working on, while he met with directors and producers to make new deals.

We shopped on Rodeo Drive so Mario could show me places that he thought I would enjoy. I love to shop, but mostly it made me feel uncomfortable. I was much more comfortable working with sick people in hospitals. It was in Malibu that I most missed being a nurse.

Still, the prices on Rodeo Drive were so outrageous that Mario and I did laugh a lot.

Whenever Mario needed to escape, we flew to Vegas to gamble. I had fun there because I could often "hear" the numbers, and we could both practice our intuition on roulette. We ate out most nights, alone or with friends.

When it wasn't raining so much that mudslides covered the Pacific Coast Highway, the weather was exquisite. Rashana made me pinky swear to walk along the shore and enjoy the sunset so that she could show me beauty in nature. She even had me listening to dolphins as they came close to the shore. Most days, I could sit on the deck watching the ocean waves crash against the sand for hours.

One day after a walk along the beach, I continued walking down Pacific Coast Highway and discovered a park with a meditation chapel.

Inside this meditation chapel, on the altar, were large pictures of many of the great Masters: Jesus, Buddha, Mohammed, Moses, even Confucius.

I slid onto one of the hard wooden benches and prayed that day, asking why I had to be such a pain in the ass when I had so much to be grateful for. The truth was I worried, I nagged, I didn't enjoy life the way I should, even though I knew it was a gift. And when I got angry, I yelled–at the people I loved and who loved me. I explained that I understood I should be incredibly happy, that I had nothing to complain about.

But the voice that answered was not God's.

"You've got to play the cards you're dealt," she said.

"Rashana, stop," I whispered. "I wasn't talking to you."

It was Eva who spoke then. "Do you not think that the soldier who hammered the nail into the hand of the Jesus had his own part in the Christ's transformation?"

Wow, I thought. I finally understood something I never had before: things aren't always what they seem, and even the most awful things that happen can be part of a perfect plan. I left the chapel feeling much better than I had when I walked in. I even waved at Ghandi's Memorial Stone as I left.

॰✵॰

Finally back in New York, I was busy editing the book, *On Wings of Truth,* getting ready to send it to the illustrator. Star Water Press Ltd. went through as an LLC corporation and I was a happy woman. As far as I was concerned, I was on my way to being a mogul–or as Mario said, a "mogirl."

I was still struggling to understand how I had been changed and thought it was a good time to check in with Dr. Canon again. After she'd welcomed me into her office, we both sat down.

"You've described the initial experience and the visions you had then. What happened immediately after that?" she asked me.

"All kinds of crazy things were going on inside my head that week. There were times that thoughts shot across the landscape of my mind like fireworks cutting through a dark night sky, and times when darkness fell like a black velvet curtain. Then one morning, another kind of collateral network seemed to kick in, almost as though someone had installed a new motherboard into my brain's computer where circuits I was unaccustomed to had been activated."

"What kind of circuits?" she asked. "How were your thoughts different?"

"Well, words began to come in frequencies, and those frequencies seemed to have numbers attached, which had meaning. I could see them, I could add them up and somehow they made sense. BABY was a three, and a three was a Godly number, and God was an eight, which was creativity and it went on and on. But when I started writing it all down on paper to make sure my addition was correct, I knew I looked like all those crazies I had taken care of. My family was worried sick, and they didn't care at all what the numbers meant. As my mother put it, 'Just stop it.'"

"There are mystical traditions that divine meaning by attaching numerical value to words, like Kaballah," Dr. Canon pointed out.

I nodded.

"There was a part of me that Eva held in witness consciousness so I could watch my actions and evaluate how far from 'normal' they were. Then with a quick shift in the gestalt, I'd find myself back in 'reality' again, knowing I had been somewhere else. It was like studying the brain and consciousness from the inside, without drugs. I felt as though I had discovered a function outside of both mind and brain, a more subtle and deeper understanding of the context in which we, as humans, lived. I was experiencing a new realm of consciousness, a space in which the mind of man touched the heart of God."

"Fascinating," Dr. Canon said.

"Yes, but as fascinating as all of that was, it was also terrifying. I was never great at 'letting go,' and letting go of my mind, which I was very attached to, threatened me with obliteration. 'I think therefore I am'—who said that?"

"Rene Descartes," she said.

"Well, what happens if I can't think? I am not?"

She laughed. "That's one interpretation. What else happened?"

"Whenever I tried to meditate, I couldn't hear Rashana at all but I could see a peridot–amethyst color begin to swirl just behind my eyes that I knew was Eva. The same way I knew a friend's voice when I picked up the phone, I recognized Eva's presence. Eva often didn't use 'voice impressions' when she was around. She used colors, changed my vision, showed me slides. She used my right brain much more than my left. And when she came in words, I knew Rashana was bridging for us. Though Eva always made a logical point, she made it a more multi-dimensional experience. Finally, I understood that there was more to me than just my mind. And I knew I existed with or without my mind."

"That's quite an insight," Dr. Canon said.

"But there was more I discovered."

One day, I was sitting on my couch looking out my big bay window. I could see the atoms making up the trees, the leaves, and the grass as energy, and it all began to move around, losing form, melting together, becoming one. It was almost like a huge snowstorm. The individual atoms, like snowflakes, flew around in front of me. All boundaries and form dissolved. I was so frightened, I covered my eyes with my hands, but I could see that my hands too were just formless energy, moving atoms. By then, I could hardly breathe, I was so terrified. I rushed into the bathroom and threw water on my face to try to get back to reality, but it wasn't enough to make me feel steady, so I grabbed a pencil and paper to try to 'draw' the landscape back into the form I remembered. Then the most amazing thing happened."

Dr. Canon was leaning forward in her chair, nodding encouragement for me to go on with my story.

"My hand resumed its solid form around the pencil as I gripped it, and as I drew the house across the street, and the fence, the trees, the grass and everything else, it all came into focus outside my window as it took shape on the page. It was as though that single action brought me back into time. Suddenly I knew that everything was made up of the same stuff, whether I called it energy, atoms, or consciousness. It was then I understood that all art was self-portrait, and that the nature of separateness on earth was both truth and illusion at once. As I settled back into the limited vision of ordinary consciousness, all I could say was, 'Thank you.' And I really meant it. The expanded vision I had prayed for my whole life had scared the shit out of me. It certainly wasn't practical in the everyday three-dimensional world."

When I finished, Dr. Cannon said, "So much of the brain is unexplored territory. We use less than 20 percent of it. There's 80 percent that's still uncharted. That's a lot left to explore and discover."

"Does that mean I'm not crazy?" I asked. "Because I sure reminded me of a lot of those people in institutions I took care of."

She smiled at me then. "I don't even know what crazy means," she said. "Certainly some of us have different perceptions than others, but different times and different cultures would call the same perceptions either sacred visions or pure madness. Maybe what you're experiencing is the new frontier."

Mario and I flew back out to Malibu. This time we rented Mel Brooks and Ann Bancroft's beach house. I loved that house. There was a room on the third floor that offered me complete solitude, to hide, and write, and to meditate for as long as I wanted. I met Shinzen Young, a meditation master, and we took long walks as he taught me walking meditation—how to develop my senses and use them to understand more of the world I lived in.

Although the ocean washed onto the shore and the beach was right out the back door, perfect for taking walks, the most pleasure I got was from the sound of the surf and the freedom to write. Still, something was not right with me, emotionally. I felt flat. So I kept writing to try to figure it out.

Dear Eva,

Why am I having such difficulty and resistance in writing the new healing book? I need to get on with it and yet I feel something is stalling me.

Dearest Guess Who,

I have the feeling that you know the answers to all the questions that you are asking but if you need them verified, then I will be happy to oblige. This is Eva, of course. Rashana is standing by to help with any information you want from her.

What is real healing and what just looks like healing? How is judgment tied to fear? Do you know? What experiences did you have that made you see things differently and what did you find out about yourself as you took your inner journeys? How has this new vision or our communication helped you live a better life if it has, and if not, why not? How many of your prayers have been answered and what was it you prayed for? In what way did Fate alter your plans and how did you adjust? These are a few questions you must answer somewhere in this book. Doesn't matter where.

Dear Eva,
You seem to be asking how I can teach what I haven't yet learned, is that right? And you seem very serious–have I done something to displease you?

*Dearest,
As long as humans learn, there is no displeasure. I am being serious because right now that is my nature. Many of my aspects are called upon at different times. At this time, humor seems to be missing because of the stress of your spirit itself. Ask Rashana why the translation is so serious. She is closer than you to the problem at this moment.*

Rashana?

*Hi Moody Blues,
I am now in the midst of prevailing upon the heavens to grant us a vacation in the middle of our book because, as I said before, balance is important for healing.*

Dear Eva or Rashana,

Why did my energy level go down so far last night when Mario asked if we could go out to dinner at La Scala, and why did I feel so depressed? I can't stand that I'm such a drip.

Dear Groovy Groundhog,

Did you not know that humans foretell a change in seasons of the heart in the same way that groundhogs do? You have heralded the end of the season of your discontent and are now moving on with the currents of change. Soon you will be funny, wise and energetic, if you can let go and let it happen. All is working the way it has been planned and foretold. You, of course, have been wasting a little time in the going backward process, but there is no problem because if you go backward far enough, you will come to the present and future again. This is a circle.
Rashana

This is Eva.
Is there something you want that you haven't asked for because you didn't know you would want it?

Dear Eva,

I would like to work longer because I am feeling the pressure to get on with my life and my books and I can't believe Rashana is asking for another vacation. I am getting excited about the possibility of writing fiction and so I would like to finish with the contracts I already have. And of course I would like all my books to be good.

Dear Carola (like Granola)
 Wholesome and good they will be. You only have to sit yourself at your screen and go for it. It will happen in the best way possible. Your body is still adjusting to the vibrational changes, and you are getting used to all that has happened. Don't push. You will understand enough as time goes on. Let it unfold instead of trying to wrench it open to discover what's inside. You will rip it and it will not be intact as it would be if it were birthed in its own time. That goes for all in life. Take it easy and smoothly, and stop judging the pace, for it will come as it should.
 Rashana is learning quite well how to pace you both. You are having a harder time because on earth there is time. Here it is pacing, that is all. You have forever, and now that you are doing creativity, this isn't the only creative thing you are doing. Trust her, she is standing by and learning to flow with the current of life on two planes. Before you were so close that it almost seemed as though you were one and the same. Now she, like a kite, can fly ahead and give you time or space to cruise up. One insight in each day is quite a lot, don't you think? Enjoy your explorations and the thoughts or things we come up with. All is fun when all is love. What are you

loving about this angel book you are publishing? Please list the things you love about it, or about being able to do it.

Dear Eva,

As in any of my books or writing, I love being able to create something from nothing. First it's only a thought, then it's words on a page, then it's a paragraph, then chapters, then it's a book. From the building of one thought on another comes something real, tangible and concrete. All from a thought.

Dear Grand Master Player,

Do you see now how the world in all its gory glory was created? This, my child, is co-creating. And that is what you love about it. Your soul purpose is truth and creativity, not quantity. Go behave like a god/goddess and plant the thoughts of change that will be carried on the warm winds of love to blow and grow into the hearts of men/women. Can that be done too slowly? Or, is it just right however it's done?
Creatively Yours,
Rashana

Dear Eva and Rashana,

Thanks for the pep talk. It does help. Actually, it does help to be able to communicate with you and have you help me make sense of life's challenges. It also feels good to know what's coming, gives me some time to get prepared. It feels like a cheat sheet on life. I'll say goodbye and move on to my book now unless you have something else to tell me.

Dear Terminator,
Funny idea that just because you're changing pages, you think we have to say "goodbye" or even "see you later." We are capable of moving right along with you and so if you are going to write your book now, we'll follow right along and see you on that page. This is one of the funnier humans, wouldn't you say, Rashana?
Yes, Eva, but she is near and dear to my heart. We'll just give her a little rope and she'll find herself.

Dear High Spirits,
How do I know you're not just in my mind despite what Dr. Canon says?

Dearest Solitary One Mind,
Try minding your own business and see if you can stop hearing us.

I really couldn't hear anything for quite a long time, then I called to them again.

See how easy it is to check out your perceptions. No want, no hear. Now onward, so we can continue to work together for the highest good of all.

Work was finally going well, I was on a roll writing and even my mood had gotten better. Then Mario decided he wanted to go to Vegas again to have some fun so I was thrown into a grand struggle. I didn't want to tear myself away from my work. It sounded ridiculous to anyone who wasn't a writer, but I asked Eva if she had any suggestions to make it easier.

> *Dearest Gambler in Life,*
>
> *Do you not want to see how others play the game? You have allowed yourself all the opportunities to explore the you that you are, and this is another aspect. Also, as was mentioned before, Rashana had put in for a vacation and so the Universe has provided one for you both.*
>
> *This is Rashana.*
>
> *I hope you will make this fun for me because then I will be able to better provide the energy that is needed for soul work. The scene you will walk into is important for our well-being and in some ways will help you see another pattern in your life. Look around and experience what you are doing and then feel what you feel before you try to explain it.*

※

While we were in Vegas, I let everything go and tried to live in the moment. I practiced my intuition while I picked my numbers for roulette, and was tickled when the ball dropped. I swore I could hear the numbers and that they came in "families." Mario swore I was crazy. But still, he agreed I was incredibly lucky.

After the weekend in Vegas, we flew back to Malibu. One morning that week, while brushing my hair after my shower, I looked in the mirror and noticed something that stopped me dead in my tracks. I saw a huge lump on my neck. I ran my fingers over it, and then I tapped around it. It had a ridge and it was irregular–not perfectly round like a cyst would be. Well, I thought, it's either cancer or Hodgkin's, or if I'm lucky, a thyroid cyst. I couldn't believe it. I thought, that's so much like life. One moment I'm rolling along feeling fine, the next I take a left turn and drive right off a cliff. Damn! I thought. I was going to have to check it out. Now my heart wasn't happy.

That afternoon I made an appointment with one of the local doctors in Malibu, but he suggested that I let it go until I got back to New York. He reassured me that even if it were thyroid cancer, it would be slow growing and the cure rate was high.

I wasn't really reassured because it didn't seem slow growing to me. It had appeared almost overnight.

Once I got back to New York, I had my family doctor check it. He wasn't quite as reassuring, and he insisted I see a specialist. In fact, he called the doctor himself. But the specialist was away in Europe and I couldn't have an appointment for a month. I was relieved I had to wait, because secretly I was hoping it would just disappear.

Still, it kept nagging at me, so I figured I would ask.

Dear Eva and Rashana,

I have been concerned about the lump in my neck. I immediately thought the worst, like Hodgkin's or thyroid cancer. Of course, it could be something benign but why would something happen to distract me at this time? I have lots to do on soul purpose. Besides, you once said that it's not up to me to make an example of myself in illness. Can I ask what's going on?

Dear Lumpectomy,

You are now in the process of smoothing out your life. It is inevitable that an occasional lump or two will develop. Why? Because Life is never completely smooth or it would not be life on earth. How can we help? By reassuring you, as we have, that each who discovers the Christ within doesn't have to suffer his martyrdom.

This is a new time—a time of joy and happiness. You keep waiting for the cut in your side and the nails in your hands for verification that you are a Christ child too. Let us assure you that even He would be doing it differently in this day. Be creative. This is a new ending, a transformation without physical destruction.

You have got to see the "letting go" as it occurs over time, for this is part of purpose too. The fact is that you must now discover the truth from the illusion (Buddha's test) in the son of God and Man story. You must help develop a new myth for you to see how powerful myth can be. Jesus' miracles and his suffering, as well as his goodness have been stressed. Now is the time of Christlike peace and joy. He didn't spend his time talking to the children about suffering–He spoke of their trust in innocence and joy. Children trust because they don't fear the same things we do. Let the old story go, and create anew.

Dear Eva,
Thank you for the insight but why do I still feel so weepy?

Dear Child of Innocence,
Giving up a myth that one has built one's life on is as saddening as giving up a part of oneself that one has trusted. Wisdom and innocence is balance and sometimes it teeters like a seesaw. In that teeter there is some fear of falling off a remembered truth. Also, as hearts grow wiser the shell that encloses one's understanding begins to crack and crumble. Sometimes the welling up of the heart is misinterpreted as pain when it is only swelling, for later it will encompass more joy.

Guilt? Guilt is a pain in the head and should be viewed as that. Heart pain is different. A lump in the throat, by the way, is a blocked heart-to-mind energy field. Tears cause lumps in the throat.

Rashana is looking forward, as usual, to your fiction work. She'd like to write some less Grimm fairy tales. Don't distract yourself. All will unfold as it should and you should not allow time for worry. It is being taken care of.

Dearest Eva,

I meditated on my neck and all I saw was an Olympian bronze medal. I don't really get it. What is life going to do to me before I earn a silver or a gold? Have I gotten all the insights I was supposed to from my lump or is there still more to go?

Dearest Hop Along Tragedy,

Fine fun visions you have gotten as was intended by Rashana. But it wasn't until she saw the dither you were in that she was able to slow down the process of your learning again. She wanted you to see how faith can change outcome and that's why she had you ask for your life. She wanted you to know that you had made the decision, that she didn't do it alone and she figured better later than never, so to speak. She gets impatient when she thinks you think of her as bullying, when all she feels she wants is communication. She is moving ahead quite quickly and wished for you to follow. She was playing hard again but when she saw your pain, she became aware of her insistence on quickening the pace of all healing.

Rashana is as quick a student on spirit level as you are on soul, and so I feel you can trust her. She seldom makes a mistake— of course, they are not called mistakes here, they are called learning opportunities. She is usually able to perceive with her spirit mind all that can be done to take advantage of a mistake to correct things and then squeeze the final bit of learning opportunity from the experience. She is missing your communication with her some of the time, and of course she would like some more playing. She loved Mickey Mouse and Goofy at the Disney playland you took her to. She thought it was funny how you called for her on the roller coaster–she enjoyed that a lot.

Have you accomplished all the visions you needed from this lump? You must ask Rashana. She will know.

Hi Rashana,
I could hang you for putting me through all this stuff again. Can't you think of an easier way to do this "learning," as you call it? Though I must admit, it was a good way for me to learn some things I never would have known about myself.

Dear Hang Glider,
I felt we were taking our pace rather slowly and that this was a good way to quicken things up. I forgot how much life means to those on earth. I thought you might just act the way you did last year and say you hadn't made any choices.

Dear Rashana,
You're being a smartass spirit right now. You know that I feel I have a lot to

do, and all that experience did was confuse me.

Dear Spindle Soul,
Did you not quickly regain your equilibrium after you got yourself into a spin? Who was there to help with that but All and me? How does one know balance unless occasionally one is off balance? Also, you seemed to be at a stalemate in some of your writing and so I was meaning to help. And I think I did. All the world on earth has some discomfort and you are a part of that life.
Best of Beauty,
Rashana

Dear Rashana,
Have I learned all I should from my lump?

Dear End Frame,
Would it not be gone if you had?

Rashana,
So what's the next step?

Dear Medical Personage,
Let us see what the blood studies show. I think especially one of them will be of interest to you. It is something you had to know and we couldn't figure out any other way to get it. You will laugh of course, if I have anything to do with it.

Rashana,
What now?

Dear Fun Loving Soul,
Tomorrow. Let's see what unfolds. In the time between, do the things you love, for if you do not have to let go of something this time, you will soon enough. I don't mean to throw you into a dither. Soon enough is a manner of speaking, but it doesn't have to do with time, it has to do with attitude and soul purpose.

Dear Rashana,
I keep feeling as though I'm missing something. I now have a stiff right arm. I believe it's some kind of tendonitis but I'm wondering what the purpose of this can be? Since I've come home from Malibu, I had to pay a large sum of money to the IRS, and they are auditing my past years' taxes; I have had to go for an ultrasound on my neck for what the specialist has determined is a cyst and a node; he did blood studies and put me on thyroid medicine; I've been contacted by the District Attorney to testify at the trial of the burglar I ran into in Mario's study last year; and I have two books due in a few months.

Dear Honky Tonk Girl,
Part of what you are not seeing is what a full life you are having. You are feeling overwhelmed by all the occurrences in your life, but you are not seeing what the cram-

ming of experiences of value at this time in your life is offering you. All on the ray of Truth would have to face the same tests as the Buddha, to learn discrimination. If he is going to be one of your heroes, don't you think you should be tried in the same way in this time that he was?

This too is a direct test of discrimination. Which will become more important to you, the positive or the negative? Watch what occupies your mind most of the time and if it's the negative then switch it and create a positive atmosphere. Also what is it you do for times of fun? What do you enjoy in the middle of your troubles? What life do you live instead of things you must do? Today you have no dates. What is it you will choose to do? Think about all you must do? That's pretty funny. No wonder your right arm is limp. I would be too if I was your right arm. As it is I'm just your higher self and the Right Way. That way is to record and live in the moment. Not for lesson knowledge but for peace. Right now you have nothing to do but go inside and check your bank account. In other words check your balance. Pretty funny, don't you think?

What is missing now in your life? Peace? You're missing something you are being offered many times a day. The lump? It's smoothing out as I see it. Not going away but then it is not time for that and time is one of the tools with which we play.

Whew! I feel as though I'm sliding down a playground slide. Right into the sands of *time. Play with all these things. They are the occurrences that you live your life through. Make notes as you live, later it will be fun to see how much of the Adventureland you have seen. Much like Disneyland. Some time in Frontierland, some time in Fantasyland, some time in Adventureland–we even provided a pirate or burglar. Tomorrowland you may create. You have had some visions of a helpful nature but keep in mind that no one will visit a Tomorrowland that looks like Yesterdayland. It's been done–so don't do it again. You and I still have many more great and good things to show and see. And of course tell.*

Now, let's see if I've covered all that you asked me to. IRS? Funny name for a overseer, part of the justice system on your earth plane. Look and see what rules they play by... and allow us to show how this will help effect balance in your house. Please remember that all of these organizations are replicas of heavenly things, and still of course have quirks or quarks in them. They are learning experiences and are only to be taken as seriously as your next step in the next moment.

There is a blue balloon reigning in the skies above your head and it says: "Welcome to the higher levels of creative thinking." Thinking isn't what it really means. It really means welcome to the levels of thought that think you. It's a place of allowance and a place of development. There can be no figuring to be done in this place because nothing has been done to figure yet. We must create and then see what we've created. Then we can figure if you'd like to play that game.

Next hope is that you put aside some of your moments to play the writing game because that will help you accomplish many of the other things that you hope to. See the front lawn. Spring is coming. New growth, new flowering of all in your yard. It is a wonderful time of blooming. Take heart, feel life and be one with it.

Your lump will be removed by means other than your own. Trust is the lesson here, and medicine. Spin yourself around past the boundaries in your life and watch your world whirl with the fresh look of a child's joy. The faster you spin the more you are one with all that is. There is no problem here. Surrender to yourself, not to other. The God within knows your truth as no other and so even the unasked questions will be answered before you ask. Your contribution? Slowly take a go at it. Consciously slow it down and see what happens. Make one thing a priority each day and do that thing to your best knowledge. Then drop that thing and do another and all the while just "be" you doing. I'll go now. I have much to be about and some things to find to do. Have a pleasant day and laugh a lot. It will help you lift your head and therefore lift your arm.
Love and Blue Lights,
Rashana the Riot

Today the specialist called, said the ultrasound showed a dense mass and that I'd have to have surgery. We scheduled it for the following week. When I was meditating, I asked again for the purpose of my lump, and I was told that in order to overcome fear one has to face it in the area where one is most vulnerable. For me of course that would be medicine. I've been a nurse and watched what disease can do. So on one hand, it's one of my faces of death, but on the other I could see the finger of judgment raised toward my own face. Another lesson. It will help me suspend judgment of how others accept being sick or having surgery when I have had the experience myself. Also, they showed me a vision of a beautiful skater on very slick ice and I knew she never would have learned to skate had she been afraid of falling and hurting herself. I wanted freedom, at least that's what I said I wanted, and I'll never be able to have that freedom if I am afraid of it.

Dear Rashana,
What about smoking before the surgery? Is it dangerous?

Dear Smoke Screen,
It is not more dangerous than many of the other things that are done in life. Is it healthy? That's another question. As you know anything done in excess has things to teach. What are you feeling when you're not smoking? How long can you tolerate feeling it, and how do you feel when you smoke?

All understandings are opportunities for growth. Will it cause you to cough more and have gunk in your lung? One doesn't have to be a spirit to answer that question. What will make you more comfortable, and what will make you well more quickly? Those are some questions that must be answered from soul level. If you are asking how it affects spirit, I must say that if spirit is on a high enough level nothing in physical affects best outcome. That has been decided well before the habit was ever begun. Are you asking if you should let go of the cigarettes now? I would say it is always time to let go of anything that has a hold on you if your goal is freedom. But that is choice.

Rashana,
How long will it take me to heal and feel better once I've had surgery?

Dearest Gross Exaggerator,
I feel it will be finished shortly and you will be able to move on to other creations of ours with more laughter and greater freedom. It will be fun to see what you will create in your life and in your books that will show the beautiful side of nature, the more joyful side, the one that has little to do with suffering except in its learning opportunities.

The night before I went into the hospital to have the thyroid lump removed, I tried to get everything in order. I ordered a private duty nurse from the hospital's nursing office, so I could get what I needed without bothering any of my family or friends to stay with me. I had long before determined that a hospital was no place to be without some kind of advocate.

Teri still had a couple of months to go before her new baby was due, so I felt it was a good time to get this over with. Still, something nagged at me. I had managed to escape being hurt by the burglar, and now I had to have my throat cut by doctors in masks. It was all too crazy!

I had asked the angels to watch over me. I asked Spirit if all would go well. Eva explained that in all cases I should remember that I was not trusting the doctors or the hospital, I was trusting the Universe so that I could expect the best outcome.

Though I didn't know it at the time, it happened as soon as I was under anesthesia. Without warning, Teri's water broke. She went into labor and had to be rushed to a different hospital in another town to give birth.

The first thing I was aware of when I opened my eyes was that I couldn't swallow. I had a tube threaded down my nose through the back of my throat and into my stomach to keep me from vomiting, because that could split the stitches on my neck. My throat was swollen almost shut, and the pressure of the swelling was making me feel as though I couldn't breathe. The IV drip for the morphine had ripped out of my arm and I was bleeding all over my bed. It occurred to me again that modern medicine was a barbaric practice but until something better was discovered, that's what I was stuck with. I struggled to try to ring the bell but I couldn't reach it. Finally, I managed to drift off to sleep because the anesthesia hadn't quite worn off yet.

Late in the afternoon, I woke up and began wondering where everyone was. I had made Mario promise not to come, because he hated hospitals and I really didn't want to have to worry about him worrying about me.

Finally, my sister, Barbara, got there, told me about Teri and the baby, and I couldn't even cry without choking. The baby was fine, she reassured me, even though she was only three pounds, but I was concerned about Teri. After Greggy's death, I knew she'd be terrified.

But I couldn't move and I couldn't call her because I couldn't yet speak. They wouldn't remove the tube because they were afraid I would be sick. Okay, breathe, trust, heal, I prayed under my breath.

Barbara left to go back to the other hospital to visit Teri and see how the baby was doing. I figured I only had a few hours before the night nurse showed up. That was a relief. I thought I had covered all the bases. I dozed off and on, but as the anesthesia wore off, I got more uncomfortable and began to thrash around. The floor nurse had called to have my IV restarted so I could have my pain medicine, but the doctor wasn't available, the hospital was busy and they were short-staffed.

Still no private duty night nurse. It was almost eleven. The hall lights were already off and there was an eerie silence. I was thrashing around, madly writing notes and ringing the bell so that the nurse could get the doctor to pull the tube from my nose. It was too uncomfortable to bear. The doctor still hadn't been up to restart the IV. My veins were small and fragile. Several IV techs had tried but my veins were hard to find, and each time they managed to find one, as soon as they put a needle in, it blew. Even the Intensive Care nurse wasn't able to get a vein. So there I was: slit throat, no medicine, no night nurse. Perfect. Later, I found out that was the good news!

It was almost midnight before the private duty nurse showed up. She came in disheveled, upset and crying. She took a moment to tell me her name was Ginger.

"What's wrong?" I wrote on the pad they had given me, noticing she looked distraught.

She paced my room, wringing her hands. "You wouldn't believe the kind of a day I had. I spent the whole day in court," she explained.

I had some sympathy for her after my experiences before the Grand Jury testifying against the burglar. I assumed it was the same for her so I grabbed my pad and wrote, "Who did you have to testify against?"

"Oh, no," she said, as she continued pacing alongside my bed, tears running down her cheeks. "I was defending myself."

"From whom?" I wrote.

"The family of one my patients and the hospital counsel. They accused me of causing one of my patients brain damage by overdosing him with too much medicine. They kept grilling me as though I was a criminal."

"Did you?" I scribbled. "Did you give him too much medicine?"

She had tears streaming down her cheeks as she explained. "I couldn't swear to anything. It was over ten years ago. He was an eight year old kid at the time, now he's a teenager in a wheelchair. I told them I couldn't remember what happened that long ago. But they wouldn't let up."

I was shaking my head repeating over and over in my head, "I'm trusting the Universe, not the doctors, nurses or hospital. Trusting the Universe."

Ginger sat on the bed, and I patted her hand to try to comfort her.

"You understand, don't you?" she asked. "You're a nurse. What do they want from me? My firstborn child? I really don't remember. I was on Pediatrics and I had to take care of so many kids that night."

This was a scene straight out of my book, *The Nurse's Story*. This was obviously another test of discrimination, another face of death. Only this time I was not in the wrong story, and this was a tougher test for me to pass.

Suddenly, Ginger gathered herself together and said with great concern, "Oh, your IV is out. We should have it put back in. And we should get that gastric tube pulled."

I nodded in agreement. But when the doctor came in, he insisted we needed to leave the tube in for a few more hours, to be sure my stomach was settled. But by then I had had it.

"No," I wrote. "I'll sign a waiver so no one can hold you responsible, but if you still refuse, I'll pull it myself. One way or another, it's coming out. I can't stand this feeling in the back of my throat. I can't breathe." I was scribbling like a crazy woman with an occasional grunt for emphasis.

The doctor wasn't happy about it but finally he agreed. As soon as that tube was out, he offered to put in a new IV. But before I allowed him to do that, I looked at Ginger and managed to croak, "What kind of medicine did you give that kid?"

"Morphine. The kid was on a morphine drip." She pointed to my IV bag. "Like yours."

I nodded. When the doctor walked over to the side of the bed, I told him, "I'm not having that much pain. I don't think I need pain medicine any more. In fact, you can forget the IV."

❦

Teri's new baby, Shari, had been born prematurely at thirty weeks. She was only three pounds, so she was still in the neonatal nursery two days later when I stopped by to see her on my way home from the hospital. She was a tiny little thing, no bigger than my palm. Her eyes were covered with black eye patches to protect them from the ultraviolet lights in the incubator and they had oxygen running through tubes in her nose. She was off the respirator, but her tiny little chest was heaving up and down with the effort of her breathing. When I reached into the incubator and put my finger in her hand, she grabbed it tight, with real strength. "Baby," I promised her, "If you stay alive for me, I'll stay around for you." She was so much smaller than Greggy was the first time I saw him, and yet while he had made me cry, Shari made me laugh.

My voice or my promise seemed to comfort her, because her chest stopped heaving and she started breathing with less effort. Before I left, I asked the neonatal nurse how she was doing. She told me the baby would need a few more days on oxygen but other than that she seemed perfect.

༺✺༻

The next few weeks were a hectic time for me. I felt awful for Teri when she had to leave the hospital without her baby and come home to an empty crib, especially after having had a baby die. She was so brutalized by the C-section for Shari that she still was not healed. Because this baby was so small, the doctor decided she had to be awake for the delivery. When Teri began to hemorrhage, everyone in the delivery room got frantic. Then, she had what could only be considered a near-death experience that saved her sanity by taking her out of her body. But while she was still in her body, she felt completely invaded. It seemed almost mythic, she said, with everyone's face covered by masks and so many hands inside her pulling her baby from her very center. She was so traumatized that she didn't tell me for weeks afterward.

During the following week I found out that the burglar I ran into in Mario's house was sentenced to 322 years in jail. Obviously he can only serve about 30 to 50, of course, but as Eva told me, he won't see freedom for quite some time. Spirit was happy to report he had finally remembered his soul purpose.

My audit was finished and everything had been done correctly.

Two weeks later when I went out to Joe Heller's house in the Hamptons with Mario, we had a good time, but when I came back my muffler fell off, big black carpenter ants were crunching through the walls in my bedroom like Rodan, the pump on my oil burner burned out, and one of my caps fell out, so I was feeling a little toothless. We seemed to have gotten over the internal malfunctions, but now the outer world was malfunctioning. All of this was going to cost a fortune to repair and I felt crazy again. So, I had another question.

> Rashana,
> Well, my life is full of change again. As you know my thyroid lump was operated on and the pathology report said there were two lumps, one behind the other. Neither was malignant, which left me with a sense I had more to do on earth.
> I thought it was kind of crummy that Teri had to have her baby in the only two days that I couldn't be with her because I was in another hospital. What kind of

spirit planning was that? I don't mean to insult you but what good is spirituality on earth and what good is doing spiritual work if life stays so difficult?

Dear Deal Maker,
The first thing you must understand, and I don't mean to insult you, is that once you ask "what good?" you're not doing spirituality, or even good works on earth, you're just doing a different kind of business. This time with spirit instead of with earthlings. The point of all is unconditional love and if you want to spare yourself suffering that includes doing things without goals. Letting go of all outcomes and just accepting all outcomes is a way to higher knowledge. The Middle Way is not the Middle Class or the Middle Income and it certainly isn't High Class or High Income. You're mixing things up again. If you lived several lives of plentitude, then why would we have you repeat the same course again? What would you learn? Did you notice, by the way, that it's in times of hardship that many people feel loved because of the help of others? Have you seen how people pull together in cases of natural disasters and unnatural ones too? Hurricanes and air crashes are destroyers of the physical, but they are creators of unity and courage in many ways. The times of your hardships help you suspend judgment of others, and help you suspend the idea that if one lives correctly, one lives well in a material and financial way.

You are not meant to be kept in a state of poverty in this life because you are to be doing happiness and joy and trying to integrate that aspect. But even here there is not as much of a correlation as you think. There are people in wheelchairs who are freer than those with healthy physical bodies, and there are people with less money happier than those with more. We are trying to teach discrimination and subtlety on your plane as well as showing the beauty in diversity. But more than that, the biggest gift that we can offer in the life of a human being or soul on earth is the "peace of mind" that cannot be bought at any price.

Rashana,
If I don't sell some of my books so I can make some money in order to help me with my family, how does this communication help?

Dear Worrisome,
If money traps, rather than frees you, it is against our soul purpose because freedom is the goal of our life this time. That is why we have to show that responsibility and guilt must be dropped before money can be achieved. You must think of ways in which money will make you freer, and not trap you. Then we can move forward as planned.

Rashana,
I'm impatient with myself and that doesn't help my creativity. Can't you

do anything about helping me out with that?

Dear Wholier Than Before,
This is the time for learning to be a priority in your own life. Please consider in a list what you have gained and what you have lost. Both of course are moving toward balance but it is always on the side of better if you can get more adds than gones. It seems that you are really enjoying the "being" side of your nature and have learned more about letting the "doing" side rest now and then, but it is necessary to keep the balance in your creative work.

The mother aspect needs to be balanced with the sister aspects for brotherhood contributions to your world, and the personal needs to be balanced with the universal.

Spirit must find balance with soul and home with travel.

In and out.

Parties and solitary time.

Learning and teaching.

Creating and watching what has been created by others.

And the overriding acceptance of a life where there is knowledge that everything is working perfectly certainly helps. We have been watching and overseeing your life and it seems that most often when you can come from your center you realize this very well. When you forget and treat spiritual things like meditating, reading and writing as "shoulds," you

overwhelm yourself again. You have lifetimes to accomplish what you must and there is no doubt that you will. Relax your worries. We are here to help always.
Lots of love,
 Rashana

Rashana,
 In the middle of all this what should I be trying to help my children learn?

Dear Troubleshooter,
 Let each find their way to the truth they must know. Encourage the search for knowledge but don't offer too many clues. The lessons they need to learn may not be as obvious as you think they are. Life is moving on and so are you in just the ultimate direction.

Dear Rashana,
 My parent's are going to be married fifty years and I'd like to give them a Golden Anniversary party. Is there another reason I feel there's purpose in this celebration?

Dearest Soul Dancer,
 It is the outside evidence of organized labor for good. Each of these parents is so different, and yet a group together like this family shows the dance that can be done when the concept of unity is stressed to the fullest.

Do you not see the purpose in the wedding of freedom and individuality (father) and of commitment to the whole with the sacrifice of personal freedom (mother)? It is the marriage of the male and female principle. It is a celebration of the god and goddess in each of us, done in a two-step for their dance. It will be a good day and a day of great rejoicing. It will also be the day that your father will realize what your mother has known all along. It will be his birthday. All sends love and celestial confetti to both.
*Lovely laughter and Light,
Rashana*

Wow! I thought we were just celebrating their endurance. Still, I should have known they had something special–after all these years, he still called her Lotus Blossom.

Dear Rashana,
I think that cleared a few things up. So thank you. Now that I know I'll be okay and have even started writing again, I should feel better. Anything else before I sign off?

*Dear Draper of the Past in Colorful Hues,
Each time you have had to learn a hard lesson you have always known it with your heart ahead of time. That does not mean that you should avoid a hard lesson. Hard lessons sometimes accomplish great growth. Also, when you can finally see what a lesson feels like for*

that aspect, you will be able to balance those undeveloped aspects as well. Please remember that in order for there to be a healing there must be a wound. Also remember that you can not release something until you are finished with it. If a book is not finished to your satisfaction, finish it as best as you can. And then, and this is the most important, Let it Go!

It is time for me to have a celestial soda pop and I suggest you go about your business. It is a happy holiday coming up for us and then we are going to see California and to gamble in Las Vegas. My number four is a good one this time.

I wish to share something with you about one of my new creations. I made an icicle today for the heavenly tree. It is of course not ice, and of course not tinsel, but it is a form of straight light that I have looped together to make a long thin bright strand that can be hung on the clouds which we are also decorating. It's hard to explain to most human livings what it is to create something beautiful that has no purpose except its beauty. And this icicle is one of the most beautiful I have ever seen. All will be pleased. Well I must fly.

Wishing you and all your earthly family, Beautiful heavenly icicles!
Rashana Claus

Suddenly, I saw the blond fairy angel and she was wearing a Santa hat and a beard. This time I knew it was Rashana. She held out a beautiful swirling icicle, a clear rainbow crystal, and offered it to me.

"Thank you," I said. Then I teased, "Still blond?" But she was gone.

❊

Mario and I spent New Year's Eve in Vegas, locked in our room watching the ball drop in Times Square instead of in the casinos where all the partying was going on. At midnight we called all the kids at home to wish them a Happy New Year. Afterwards both of us made our list of resolutions. I vowed to work less. Mario vowed to work more. Balance, perfect. The following day I sat to write again.

> Dear Rashana,
> Well, here it is the beginning of a New Year and I wanted to take the opportunity to tell you that I'm ready to start working with you in the best and most cooperative way that I'm able to. Though I am still working on the healing into death book, I want you to know I would like to consider your need for beauty and joy.
>
> *Dear Haunted Soul,*
> *I can help you with the questions about the Truth of the transition human livings call death, because questions about Truth are one of the choices that is in my spirit purpose. If you can hear what Eva answers as Truth, then you may be able to turn your healing books around and make them lighter books. One of the questions is: Why do you want*

to write these books? And what do you hope to accomplish? How much are you willing to blow through the tunnel of time to reach the truth you are after? Are you willing to trust Eva and All enough to take your chances on a truth that you do not yet know? You must go forward toward tomorrow with a vision of a truth you have not arrived at yet.

Eva wishes to speak...

Dear Student Healer,

Here is something that you have not considered enough: the way in which we can help you ask the proper questions. Answers are not always the most important dynamic of a situation.

Why do you trust Life? Is it because nature built more trust into your genes? Is it because in your early environment, trust was one of the issues you learned? Or was the truth of Death already written on your soul from previous lifetimes?

I must say this about arriving at the door of Death: It is a gradual and familiar landscape for those who have been there. It is recognizable as a place of homecoming if the person has been there before. If not, the altered state of the landscape is frightening in a surrealistic way, especially for one who cannot remember the visions of castles from childhood. The quality of the colors is brighter and more fluid and the ground moves beneath one's feet. That allows for less chance of getting stuck. Do you have a very special question you would like to ask?

Dear Eva,
What kind of healing book will be of the highest good in helping other human beings?

Dear Carol,
Helping in what way?

Dear Eva,
Helping me and other human beings approach death and healing as an adventure rather than with dread, and also helping all of us accept the fact that we are all being taken care of in ways that we can't yet understand.

Dearest Cause You Can,
What's the vision in your heart right now?

Dear Eva,
A can of honey salve.

Dear Nurse,
Will that help?

Dear Eva,
Not really. Except for a "be" sting.

Dear Soul,
Come up with something more creative.

Dear Rashana,
   Can you help?

Dear Funny Sights,
   Here goes. Can you not see a gun that shoots stars? Can you not see a Fourth of July firecracker? Can you not see a baby, or a Maypole celebration? Can you not see a heart that's been mended? A soul that's been saved? Can you not see yourself in another?

Dear Spirit,
   But that's my truth. Is it the real Truth?

Dearest,
   There are not different Truths on Higher Levels. There is One. Go and seek and find, with joy. This is an awesome feat and when you see how simple it is, you too will laugh.

Dear Rashana or Eva,
   I would like to show humans the value of a belief system that reaches to the depths of the soul in alleviating fear and allowing for growth and joy in life. I would like to accomplish that.
   I would like them to understand that all healing begins on a spirit level, not on the physical level, and that it reaches into more subtle issues in sickness, health and healing. I would like to show that unconditional love heals everyone, but that it's really difficult,

as a human being, to come from that place of Love.

My Dear Little Soul,
Understand here what you are saying. The vibration of Fear is a far easier vibration to tune in to than the vibration of Love that you speak of. This is Eva, of course. One true focus here must be on unity and non-specialness. Where there is to be healing, "specialness" must be overcome and the understanding of how special "ordinary" is, must be stressed. It must be shown that in the group mind of ordinariness, there is something very special.

Dearest Eva,
What is the truth that I have to blow through time to get to?

Dear Caring Soul,
The Truth of the Nature of Oneness.

Beautiful Dreamer,
Rashana here. I have a wish for you to indulge, if you are able. There is a dream communication I have been waiting to practice if you don't mind.

Dear Rashana,
What do you need me to do? I haven't been remembering any dreams I've had for months now. Even if I get it, I might forget it before I even wake up.

Dearest Forget Me Not,
 If you can see it, dream it, and remember it, will you write it? For me?

༺❦༻

I fell asleep that night with the promise to Rashana on my mind, with the intention of allowing her to give me the gift of her vision. Almost instantly Rashana was standing on a cloud in front of me doing her usual "Cloud Dance" step, a cross between aerobics and disco dancing. As soon as I realized she was there, in my dream, I asked, "Can I help you with something?"

She stopped dancing, and her loose fitting light blue gown fell softly around her small feet. Her long, silky hair was still blond. "Want to play?" she asked.

"Sure," I said. "I'd love to."

"I have a gift for you," she said with a smile that was both mischievous and angelic.

I was wary. "What kind of a gift?" I asked her then.

She raised her hand, in which she held a golden wand. She began to blow bubbles through the gold ring she held high in front of her. Beautiful rainbow colored bubbles filled the sky. She smiled at me, obviously pleased with herself. Then she reached for one of the larger bubbles and as she touched it, it seemed to turn into a smooth, round, rosy quartz crystal. She tossed it at me playfully. And I, thinking it would be hard, put my hand up to block it–which sent it spinning back to her. Like a beach ball, she tossed it again. This time I threw it back.

"Come be with me," she said, as she ran toward the beautiful blue water that seemed to open like an ocean in front of her.

"I can't swim," I told her.

"I can," she said laughing.

By some magic of heart and mind, I was able to follow her as she swam underwater. I watched as she rolled herself into a ball and went spinning downward, downward, deep. I could see her as she wove coral and shells through her hair. The bubbles she blew while underwater looked more like the small fine soda bubbles than the bubbles I had blown the few times I swam.

"Why are yours different?" I asked.

"Spirit breath causes the silver shimmer on the waves," she explained, as though I should have known. Then with her head thrown back and her arms raised in front of her, she seemed to arc upward until she broke through the surface of the water and was back in the sky. Once there, she reached for some of the smaller bubbles she had blown and wove them into a rosy quartz necklace. When she came toward me again she was holding it forward, and when she reached me she placed it around my neck.

"Thank you," I said.

"Would you like to come with me?" she asked.

She took me by the hand, and suddenly I could feel my head spinning. "I'm dizzy," I told her.

"Well, open your eyes," she said, "and look down."

Beneath me I could see my house, and my car in the driveway. "I feel like I'm flying," I told Rashana as the world below me fuzzed.

"What do you see?" she asked.

"Small well-kept houses, green grass and trees," I told her. And as we flew over town, I said, "I can see the lanterns that line the streets, the tall pine on the triangle and the new signs on all the storefronts."

"Quite beautiful, isn't it?" Rashana asked.

"It is," I agreed, and I tried to remember when I had ever seen it looking so green and lush.

"Can we continue?" she asked, looking sideways at me. Now we were flying side by side like Peter Pan and Wendy.

I looked down just as we passed over a very poor district in Mexico. Dark-haired children with ragged clothing were sitting on fallen stoops outside ramshackle huts, looking forlorn. We flew quickly, the scenes below almost a blur.

Next we flew over Haiti, the area of the devastating earthquake, and I could hear the cries of the people reaching high into the sky. I put my hands over my ears and then over my eyes. When I opened them again we were just going over India, Calcutta to be exact. And now Rashana pointed down at a group of children and old people in rags squatting on one of the sewage-filled gutters. "Those people have come to learn about suffering," she said, simply. "They have chosen very difficult incarnations so that they can learn as much as possible. Some of the poor areas in Mexico, some of the devastated areas of Haiti, some of the most restrictive areas of fire and floods in Russia provide the opportunities for excellent learning about suffering."

She said it with compassion, but still I didn't know what she was getting at. Soon, we flew into New York and I recognized the area of Long Island around my house.

Suddenly, we were back in my living room, sitting across from each other on the rug. Rashana asked, "Why is it you wish to do suffering?"

I'm afraid I was a little snappy. "I don't *wish* to do suffering, as you put it. I'm trying to show the difficulties that all human beings have in the crisis times of their lives," I said.

"The joyful areas of life are not written enough about," she said. "Beauty is not as trivial as you think it to be."

"I don't think it's really trivial," I said, trying to make her feel better. She'd sounded discouraged.

"If a soul constantly takes on too many heavy incarnations," she explained, "it becomes stuck in suffering. It batters the Spirit. To reach harmony and balance, it is necessary to do some serious joy."

"That's what you do?" I asked, thinking to myself she didn't have a clue about life on earth.

I saw her frown and then she shuddered. "I will tell you it's not an easy thing to do "Joy" having you as a soul. You make everything harder than it has to be."

"Sure," I said, "It's easy for you to talk when you don't have anything to do but play. I have important work to do, things that will help evolution, things that will help raise consciousness, things that will help save the planet."

Rashana looked shocked. "That's what you think you're doing?" she said. "Well, it's clear I haven't done the job of teaching you humility," she said. "Talk about work..."

"Don't try to pacify me by changing my focus," I said, "What do you do all day or time or whatever?"

She seemed to be studying me. Then in a very unspiritlike fashion, she lifted me up by the scruff of my neck and started flying with me again.

"Where are we going?" I asked, startled.

"To my place," she said. "So I can try to make things clearer."

The wind blew in my face and in my hair, sometimes so hard it took my breath away.

"How much longer?" I managed to sputter out.

"Until we get there," she said in a firm voice.

Then suddenly it seemed as though she dropped me down on a cloud. All around there was just swirling white energy, some of it a thicker white than the rest. "Stand up," she said, and grabbed me by the hand.

I struggled to my feet and she began to float across the cloud floor. "Nice clouds," I said.

"Thank you," she said, but there was a chill in her voice.

Up ahead I saw what looked like an igloo. "That's where you live?" I asked, as we walked toward it.

"I live everywhere," she said. "I'm sure I've told you that before. This is just where I formulate my plans."

"It seems pretty stark to me," I said, as I bent low enough to get through the doorway. Rashana seemed not to notice and just walked right in, as though nothing were in her way.

Inside, in the center of the one large room, there stood a large shiny telescope. "What's that for?" I asked.

"Besides humility, it couldn't hurt if you learned some patience," she said. "I'm about to explain."

She walked over to the telescope and beckoned to me to come. Then she told me to put my eye against the scope. Wow! I thought. Right in front of the lens, there was a beautiful young woman from Siam, dressed in brightly colored green and magenta robes, dancing the most graceful dance I had ever seen. When she stopped dancing, she seemed to walk toward me. I could see her bright black eyes and long dark lashes. She had smooth bronze skin, a fine nose and very full, well-defined lips painted with a bright crimson red. "She's really pretty," I said. "Who is she?"

Rashana walked up alongside me and said, "Please turn the scope slightly to the left."

When I did, I could see a tall good-looking man dressed in a pirate's outfit, complete with a black patch over his right eye. He was fencing with someone I couldn't see. "Who's he?" I asked Rashana.

But all she said was, "Turn the telescope a little more to the left."

I saw a caveman dressed in animal skins waving around a club made of thick bumpy white wood. A really ugly creature, I had to admit. "I know," I said. "I know, just turn the scope a little to the left."

Rashana giggled for the first time.

This time there was an Indian, a tall dark, dancing Indian with feathered headdress and leather moccasins tied up along his calves. I could hear the cry, the high-pitched call of war.

Without asking now I again looked through that telescope, turning and turning it until I'd made almost a complete circle. At every stop there was a different time, a different person, a different outfit, a different culture, a different face. Finally, back almost to where I started again, I asked Rashana, "Who are all of those people? Why are they here and what do they have to do with us?"

She touched me then, tenderly on the cheek. "I want you to look one more time," she said. "And tell me what you see."

I turned back and looked again through the long telescope. There was a little girl, far in the distance. "I can't see her," I told Rashana. "She's too far away."

Rashana walked up to the front of the telescope and twisted the lens. "Let me see her eyes," I said, "Zoom in on her a little more. Ask her to turn toward me?"

When she did, I gasped. Her eyes were my eyes! "Oh my God," I said, "I know her!"

Rashana smiled. "You should," she said.

"Well, who were those others?" I asked.

"My other souls from other lifetimes, your past and future lives," she explained.

"Why are they here?" I asked.

Rashana looked at me, bright stars in her eyes.

"I'll show you," she said. "Hang on."

She lifted me again, this time by the hand, and we flew until we were high above the igloo. "Look down," she said. "Look now." In a flash, all those people I had just seen and many others were transformed into a perfect circle of graceful rosy quartz crystal charms, except for one.

I pointed down to it. "That's me, right?" I said.

"That's you," she said.

The circle of small statues was too beautiful to imagine. It shined with a warm rose glow, each perfect little charm completely different from the rest and yet those very differences made it all the more intricate, all the more hypnotic.

"It's really beautiful," I said to her, softly. "But what will you do with it?"

Suddenly, we were on our way down again, down, down, down, and by the time we were ready to land, we were almost in my bedroom again.

"What was that?" I asked again.

She stood in front of me, her head held high but her voice trembling, "It's a gift I've created," she said, "It's a necklace for the Lord." She was quite breathless.

"Well, I think the Lord will be very pleased and touched by it," I said. "When will you offer it?"

Rashana put her head down and I could see a tiny bright jewel of a tear falling from her eye. "That's the challenge," she said.

"What?" I asked. "What's the challenge?"
She looked straight at me. "It has no clasp."
I remembered back, the picture of the beautiful rosy quartz necklace now etched in my mind's eye. "Oh," I said. I pondered it for a moment. "Why?" I asked, "Where's the clasp?"
She was biting her bottom lip, her eyes closed tight as though she were wishing when she explained, "I have never been able to earn one. I need one soul, in one lifetime, to reach freedom. That's what I need."
Now I was frowning.
Rashana looked at me, pleadingly.
"That's my part?" I asked, but I didn't really expect an answer. I looked at her, could see how much she wanted it. "Rashana," I said. "What were you thinking? What kind of planning was that? You need one soul in one lifetime to reach freedom and you choose me, you choose now? You send me down as a Catholic, the oldest child in the middle of a big enmeshed Italian family?"
Rashana smiled. "I know. Wasn't that a perfect plan?"
"Not really," I said.
She sighed, deeply. "It's a gift I've been waiting to give for so long."
"So that's my purpose? To get free?" I asked.
"For a gift to be truly a gift, it must be freely given," she said. "And for a soul to be free, it must also be true."
I shook my head. "You keep adding things," I said. But she looked so hopeful, I lost my head and said, "I'll try."
Rashana blinked her long silken lashes.
"Okay. I'll really try."
Rashana kissed me then, a soft gentle kiss of gratitude. She sounded excited when she added, "You never asked when I started it."

"Sometime before Christ, right?" I said.

Rashana smiled, a sweet poignant smile. "I began that beautiful rosy quartz necklace long before Christ and even longer before Time. I began that necklace on the day I began–and until this very moment I had no hope of ever finishing it."

The vision of the beautiful quartz necklace now danced before my eyes, the delicate little charms, radiant, in perfect form. I pictured it then with a clasp of pure gold. It touched me, humbled me, and brought tears to my eyes.

"Here's hoping," I prayed.

"Here's healing," Rashana said. And the last sound I heard before I woke up was the sound of tinkling crystal.

THE END